DAZED AND CONFUSED

Words and Music by
JIMMY PAGE

4

Lots of peo - ple talk - in', few of them know; soul of a wom-an was cre - at - ed be - low.

2. You hurt and a -

bused, tell-in' all of your lies; run 'round sweet ba-by, Lord, how they hyp-no - tize.

N.C.

Sweet lit - tle ba - by, I don't know where you've been; gon-na love you, ba - by, here I come a -gain.

f

B

3. Every day I work so hard bringin' home my hard-earned pay;
   Try to love you baby, but you push me away.
   Don't know where you're goin', I don't know just where you've been;
   Sweet little baby, I want you again.

4. Been dazed and confused for so long it's not true;
   Wanted a woman, never bargained for you.
   Take it easy baby, let them say what they will;
   Will your tongue wag so much when I send you the bill?

HOW MANY MORE TIMES

Words and Music by
JIMMY PAGE, JOHN PAUL JONES
and JOHN BONHAM

Moderately fast Blues

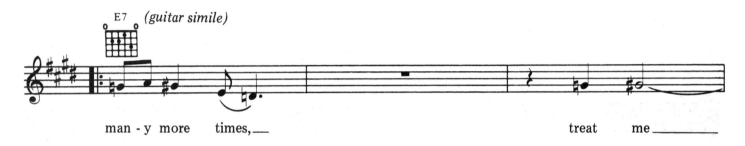

1. How

man-y more times, ___ treat me ___

___ the way you wan-na do? ___

How man-y more times, ___ treat me the

way you wan-na do? ___

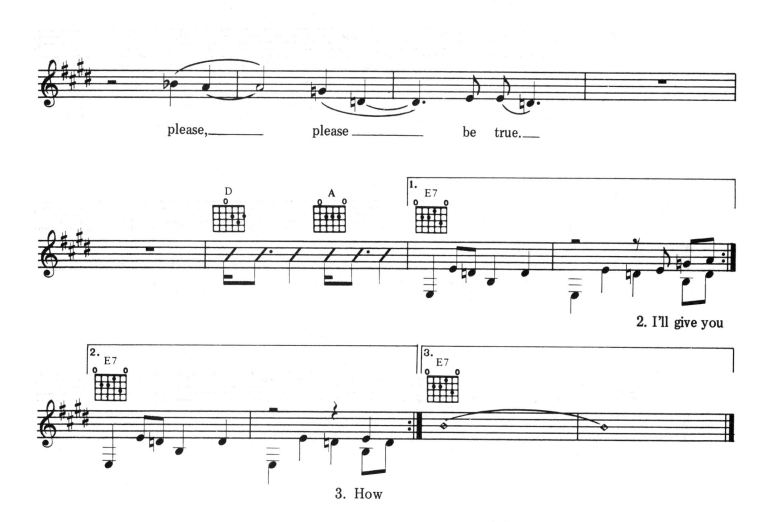

When I give you all my love, ___

please, _____ please _____ be true. ___

2. I'll give you

3. How

2. I'll give you all I've got to give: rings, pearls and all;
   I'll give you all I've got to give: rings, pearls and all.
   I've got to get you together, baby, I'm sure, sure you're gonna crawl.

3. How many more times, barrelhouse all night long?
   How many more times, barrelhouse all night long?
   Well, I've got to get to you, baby, oh, please come home.

BABE, I'M GONNA LEAVE YOU

Words and Music by
JIMMY PAGE, ROBERT PLANT
and ANNE BREDON

Moderately

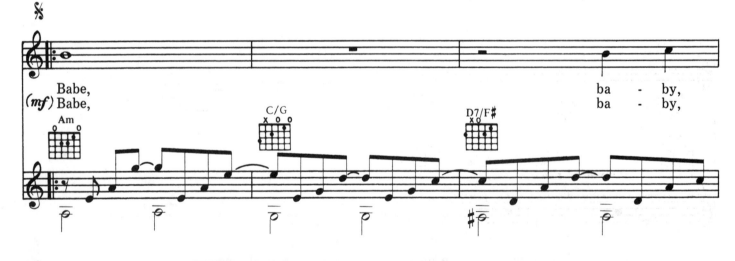

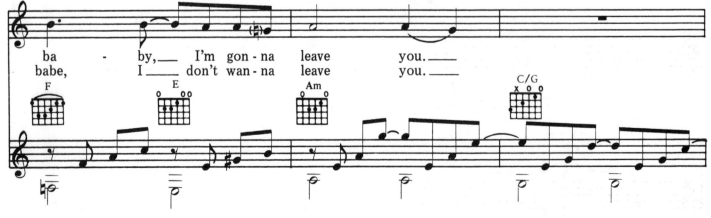

COMMUNICATION BREAKDOWN

Words and Music by
JIMMY PAGE, JOHN PAUL JONES
and JOHN BONHAM

Moderately fast Rock beat

Hey, girl,___ stop what you're do - in'.___
Hey, girl,___ I got something I think you ought to know.

Hey, girl,___ you'll
Hey, babe,___ I wanna

drive me to ru - in.___ I don't know what it
tell you that I love you so. I wan - na

is I like a - bout you, but I like it a lot.___
hold you in my arms, yeah.___

Oh, to let__ me hold you, let me feel your lov-in' charms.__
I'm never gonna let you go 'cause I like your charms.__

Com-mu-ni - ca - tion break-down,

it's al - ways the same._____ I'm hav-in' a ner -

vous break-down, drive me in-sane._____

Repeat and fade

GOOD TIMES BAD TIMES

Words and Music by
JOHN BONHAM, JOHN PAUL JONES,
JIMMY PAGE and ROBERT PLANT

Moderately slow Rock beat

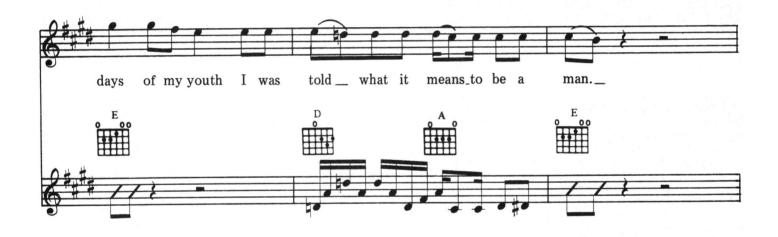

wom-an left home with a brown-eyed man, well, I still don't seem to care.

B   A   E   B   No chord

Six - teen, I fell in love with a girl as sweet as could be. It

F#   E   F#   E

on - ly took a cou-ple of days till she was rid of me. She

F#   E   F#   E

swore that she would be all mine and love me till the end. But

F#   E   F#   E

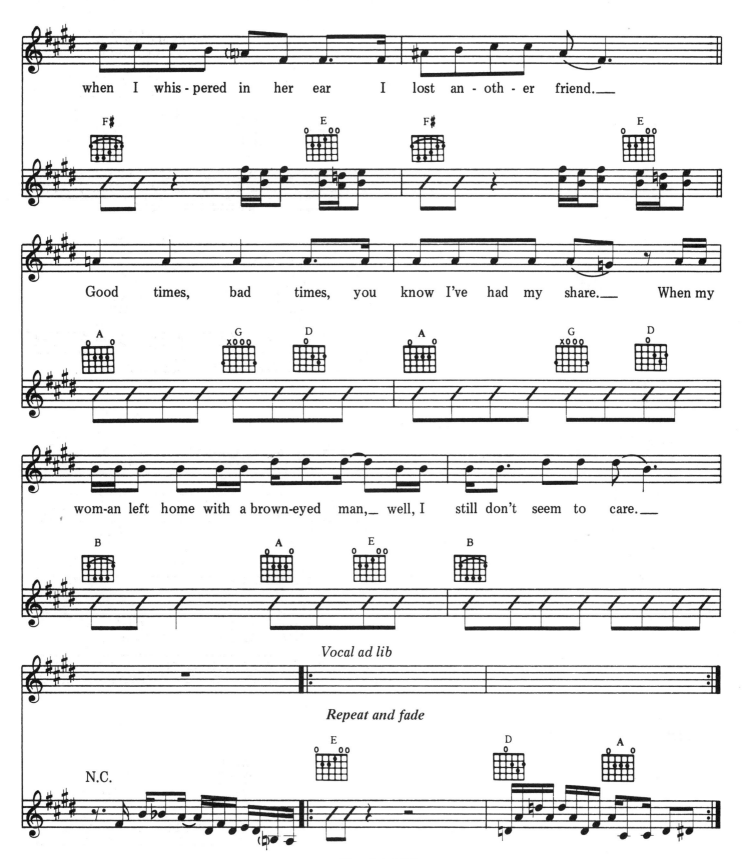

Vocal Ad Lib

I know what it means to be alone.
I sure do wish I was at home.
I don't care what the neighbors say,
I'm gonna love you each and every day.
You can feel the beat within my heart.
Realize, sweet babe, we ain't never gonna part.

YOUR TIME IS GONNA COME

Words and Music by
JIMMY PAGE and JOHN PAUL JONES

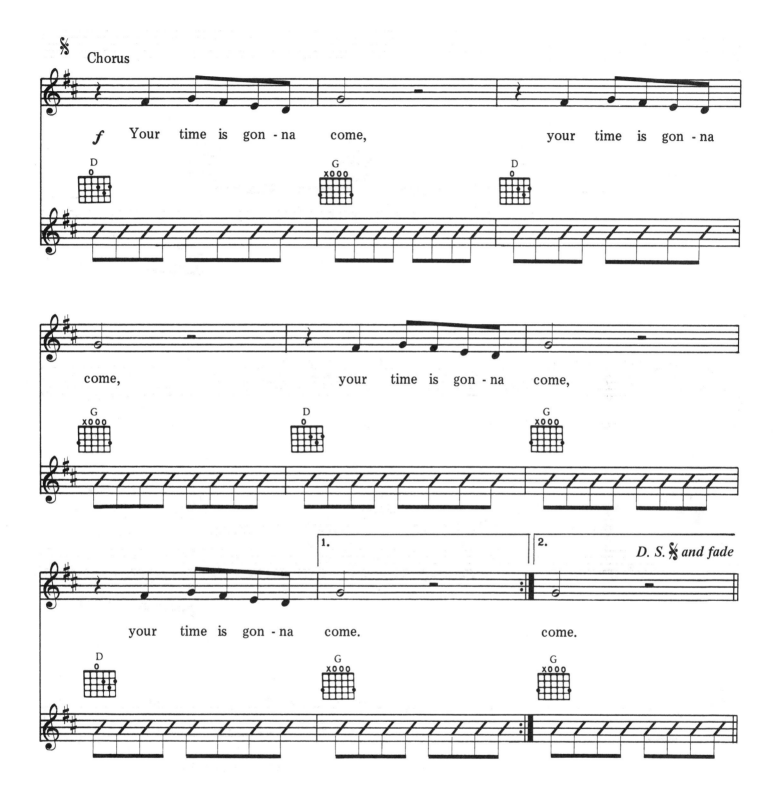

2. Made up my mind to break you this time, won't be so fine, it's my turn to cry.
   Do what you want, I won't take the brunt, it's fadin' away, can't feel you anymore.
   Don't care what you say 'cause I'm goin' away to stay, gonna make you pay for that great big hole in my heart.
   People talkin' all around, watch out woman, no longer is the joke gonna be on my heart.
   You've been bad to me woman, but it's comin' back home to you.

   (Chorus)

BLACK MOUNTAIN SIDE

Music by
JIMMY PAGE

Moderately

* Tuning: DADGAD

LED ZEPPELIN II

WHOLE LOTTA LOVE

Words and Music by
JIMMY PAGE, ROBERT PLANT,
JOHN PAUL JONES and JOHN BONHAM

Slow Blues

You need

cool - in'; ba - by, I'm not fool - in'.___ I'm gon - na

say it, yeah;___ go back to school - in'.___

Way down in - side,___ hon - ey, you need it.

I'm gon - na give you my love, __ I'm gon - na give you my love. __

Wan - na whole lot - ta love? _____ Wan - na whole lot - ta love? _

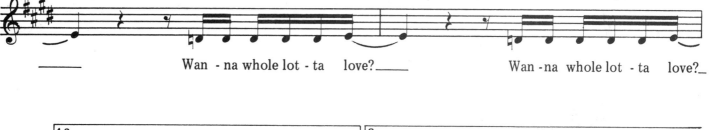

_____ Wan - na whole lot - ta love? _____ Wan - na whole lot - ta love? _

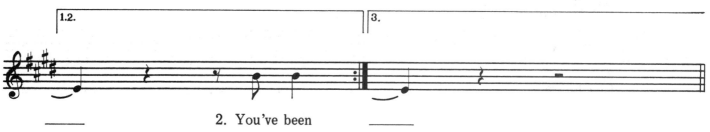

_____ 2. You've been _____

Repeat and fade

E7

2. You've been learnin', baby, I mean learnin'.
All them good times, baby, I've been yearnin'.
Way down inside, *(etc.)*

3. You've been coolin'; baby, I've been droolin'.
All the good times I've been misusin'.
Way down inside, *(etc.)*

HEARTBREAKER

Words and Music by
JIMMY PAGE, ROBERT PLANT,
JOHN PAUL JONES and JOHN BONHAM

Slow Blues

Hey   fel - las have you heard the news?___ You know that
It's   been ten years and may - be more ___ since I

28

Work so hard I can't un - wind, get some mon - ey saved. A -

buse my love a thou - sand times, how - ev - er hard I try. ___

Heart - break - er your time has come, can't take your e - vil ways.

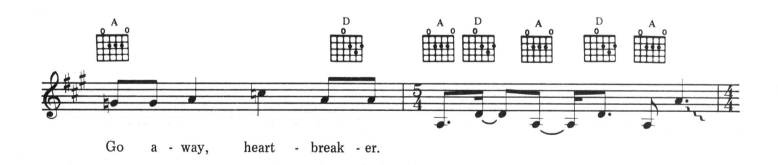

Go a - way, heart - break - er.

LIVING LOVING MAID
(She's Just A Woman)

Words and Music by
JIMMY PAGE and ROBERT PLANT

Moderately

With a pur-ple um-ber-el-la and a fif-ty-cent hat,___
Al-i-mo-ny, al-i-mo-ny, pay-in' your bills,___
Tell-in' tall tales of how it used to be,___
No-bod-y hears a sin-gle word you say,___

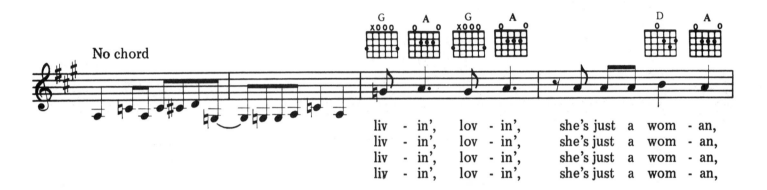

No chord

liv-in', lov-in', she's just a wom-an,
liv-in', lov-in', she's just a wom-an,
liv-in', lov-in', she's just a wom-an,
liv-in', lov-in', she's just a wom-an,

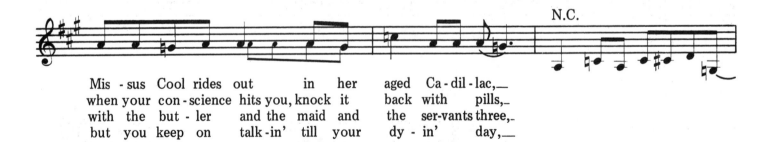

Mis-sus Cool rides out in her aged Ca-dil-lac,___
when your con-science hits you, knock it back with pills,___
with the but-ler and the maid and the ser-vants three,___
but you keep on talk-in' till your dy-in' day,___

N.C.

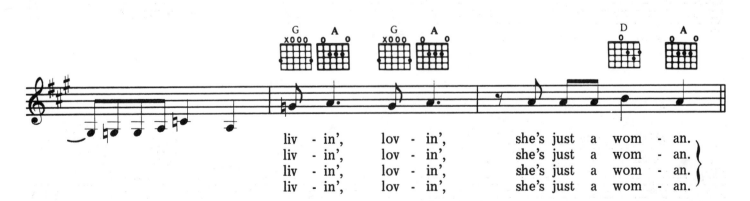

liv-in', lov-in', she's just a wom-an.
liv-in', lov-in', she's just a wom-an.
liv-in', lov-in', she's just a wom-an.
liv-in', lov-in', she's just a wom-an.

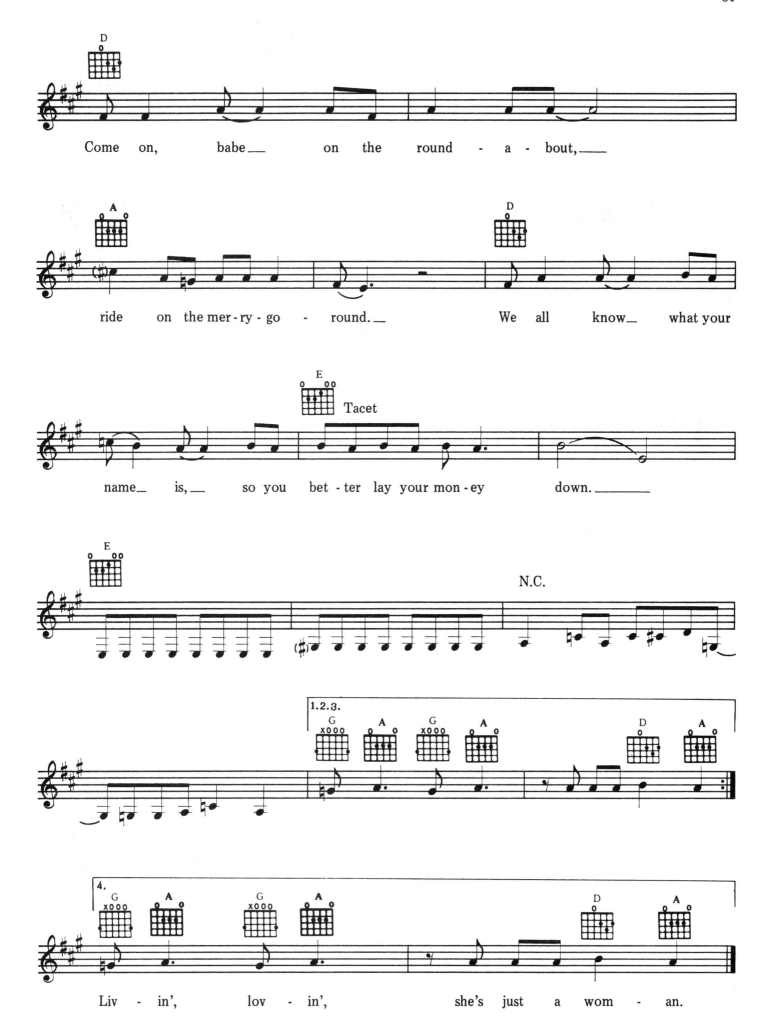

RAMBLE ON

Words and Music by
JIMMY PAGE and ROBERT PLANT

Moderately slow

Leaves are fall - ing all a - round;
Got no time to spend in route;
Mine's a tale that can't be told;

the
my

time I was on my way.___
time has come to be gone.___
free - dom I hold dear.___

Thanks to you I'm much o - bliged
And though our health we drank a thou - sand times,
How years a - go in days of old

for such a pleas - ant stay. _____
it's time to ram - ble on. _____
when mag - ic filled the air. _____

But now it's time for me to go; ____ the
Instrumental _____
'Twas in the dark - est depths of Mor - dor I

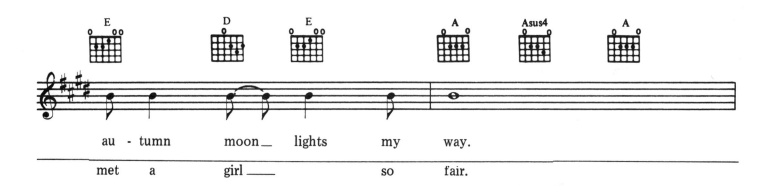

au - tumn moon ___ lights my way.
met a girl ____ so fair.

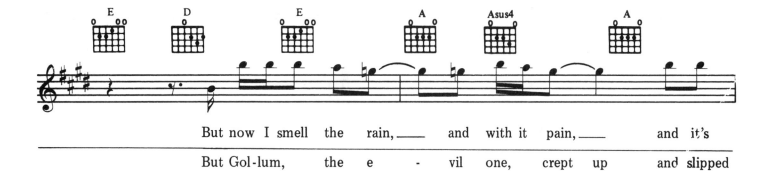

But now I smell the rain, ____ and with it pain, ____ and it's
But Gol-lum, the e - vil one, crept up and slipped

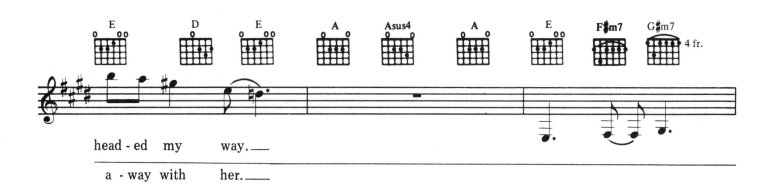

head - ed my way. ____
a - way with her. ____

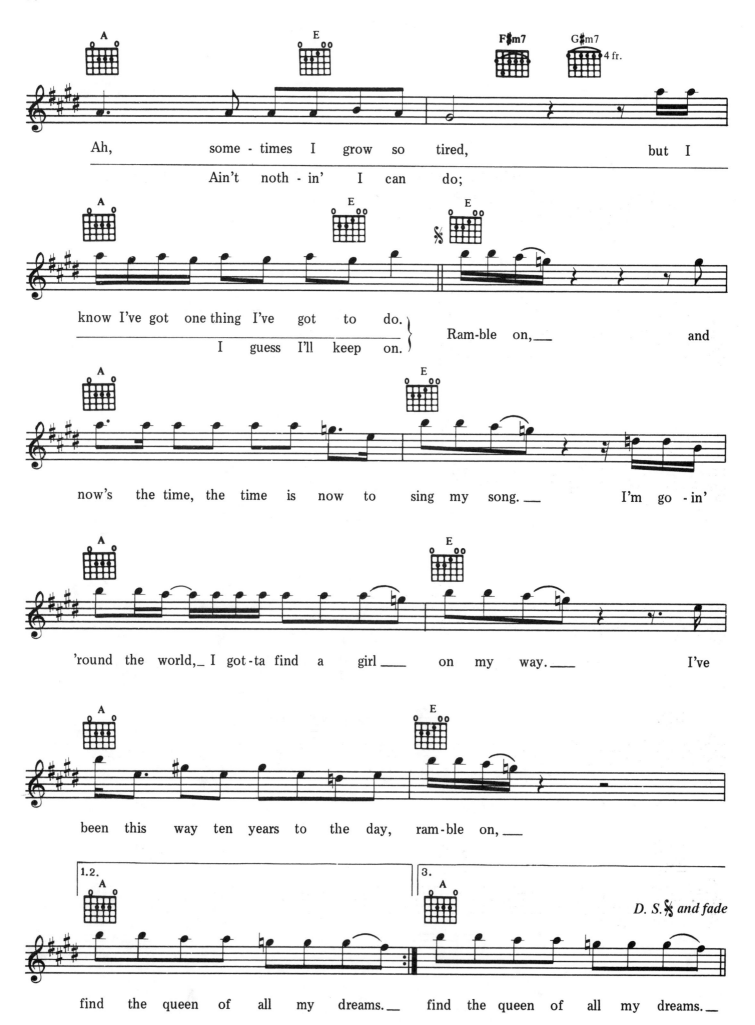

THANK YOU

Words and Music by
JIMMY PAGE and ROBERT PLANT

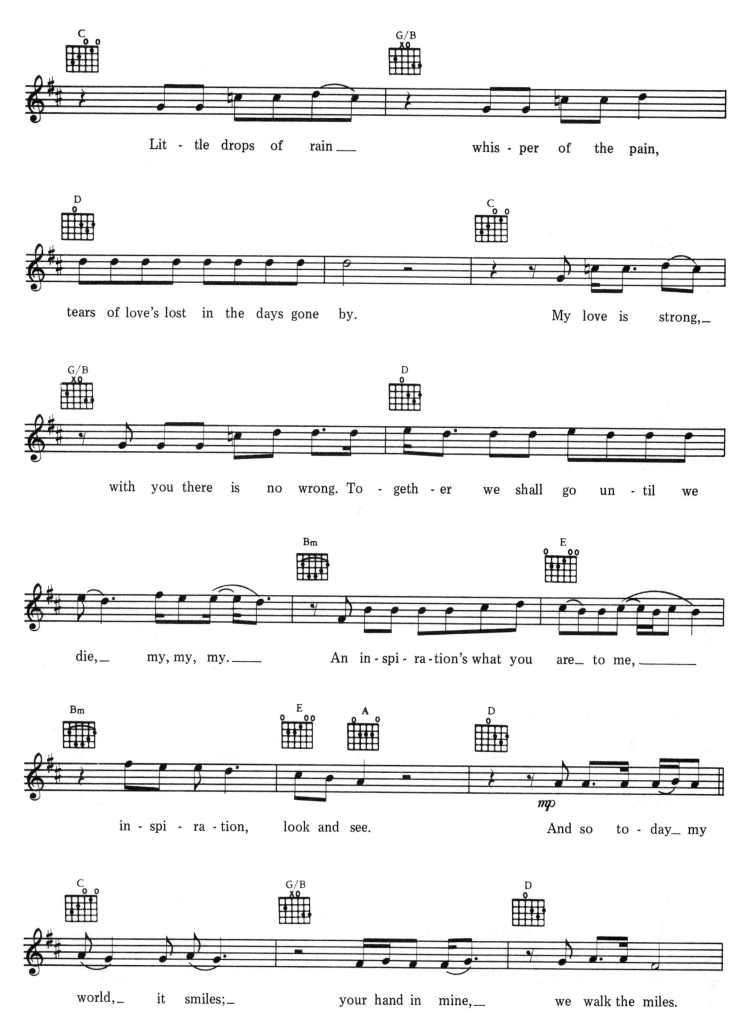

But thanks to you   it   will__ be done,__   for you to me__ are the

on - ly one. _____

Hap - pi - ness,   no   more__ be   sad;__

hap - pi - ness,__   I'm__ glad.   If   the   sun re -

Coda *Repeat and fade*

If   the   sun re -

MOBY DICK

Music by
JOHN BONHAM, JOHN PAUL JONES
and JIMMY PAGE

WHAT IS AND WHAT SHOULD NEVER BE

Words and Music by
JIMMY PAGE and ROBERT PLANT

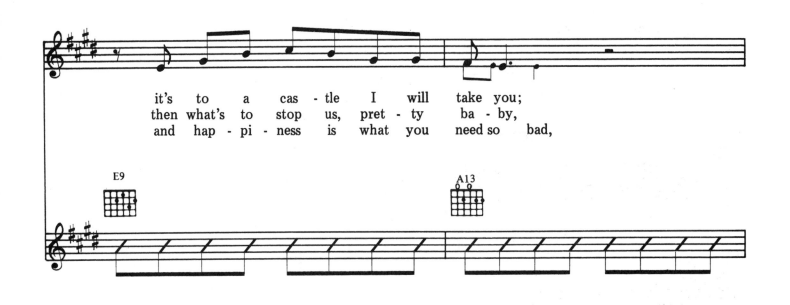

it's to a cas - tle I will take you;
then what's to stop us, pret - ty ba - by,
and hap - pi - ness is what you need so bad,

E9   A13

well, what's to be, they say, will be. ___
but what is and what should nev - er be. ___
girl, the an - swer lies with you, yeah. ___

E9   A13

Catch the wind, see us spin, sail a - way, leave to - day, way up high in the sky. ___   Then the

mf

A   A/G   F#m7   D   A

wind won't blow, you real-ly should-n't go, it on-ly goes to show___ that

A/G   F#m7   D   A

you will be mine___ by tak-in' our time.___ Ooh!_____

B   B/A   G#m7   E   B   F#

1.

And if you say to me to-

A6   mp

Tacet

2.

So if you wake up with the

mp

3.

LED ZEPPELIN III

THAT'S THE WAY

Words and Music by
JIMMY PAGE and ROBERT PLANT

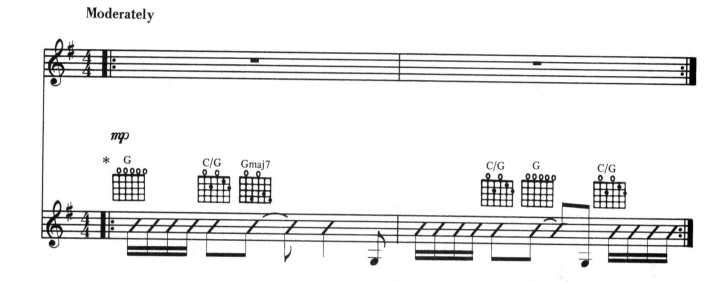

I don't know how I'm gon - na   tell   you   I can't play with you no
And yes - ter - day I saw you standing by the river,   and weren't those tears that filled your

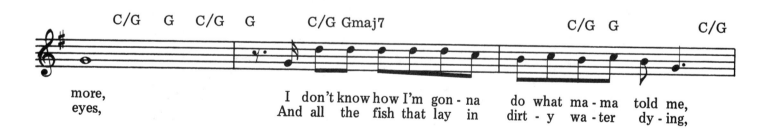

more,   I don't know how I'm gon - na   do what ma - ma   told me,
eyes,   And all   the fish that lay in   dirt - y wa - ter dy - ing,

my   friend, ___ the   boy next   door.
had   they got you hyp - no - tized?

* Use open G tuning: DGDGBD.

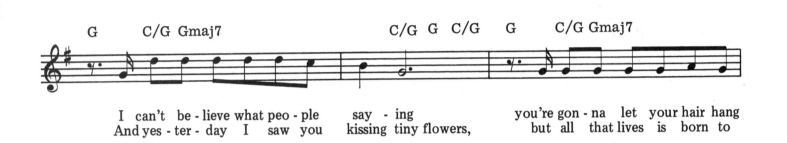

I can't be-lieve what peo-ple say-ing
And yes-ter-day I saw you kissing tiny flowers,

you're gon-na let your hair hang
but all that lives is born to

down,
die,

I'm sat-is-fied to sit here work-ing all day long,
And so I say to you that noth-ing real-ly matters,

you're on the dark-er side of town.
and all you do is stand and cry.

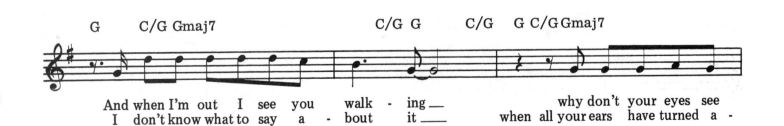

And when I'm out I see you walk-ing ___
I don't know what to say a - bout it ___

why don't your eyes see
when all your ears have turned a -

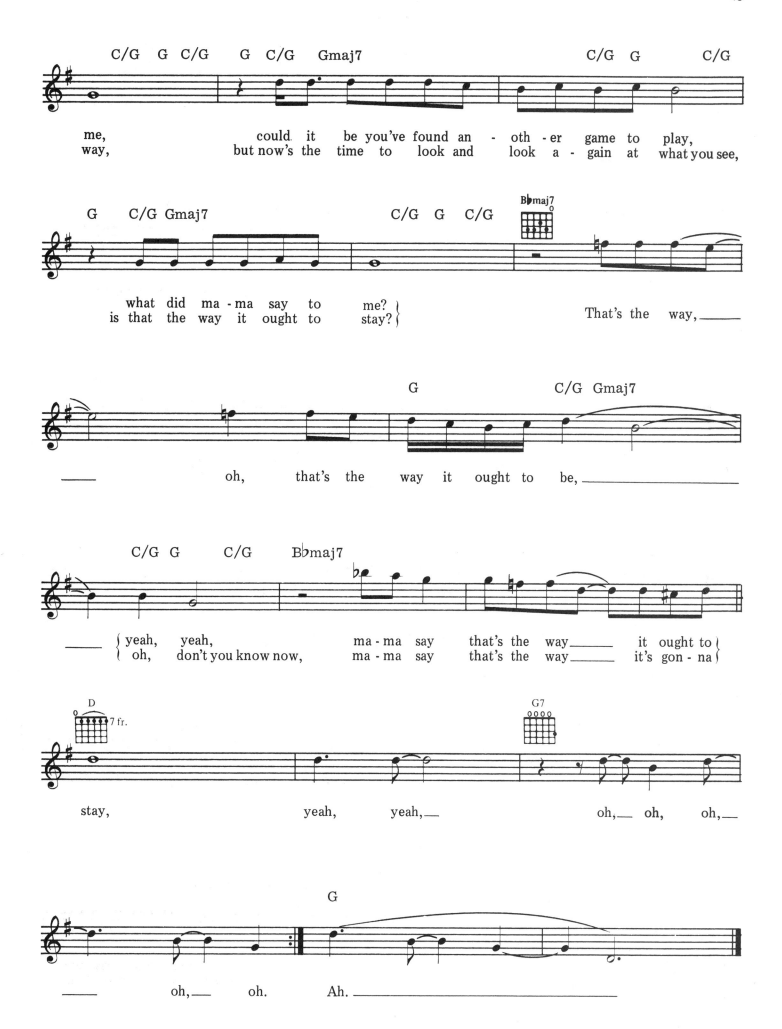

IMMIGRANT SONG

Words and Music by
JIMMY PAGE and **ROBERT PLANT**

SINCE I'VE BEEN LOVING YOU

Words and Music by
JIMMY PAGE, ROBERT PLANT
and JOHN PAUL JONES

Slow Blues

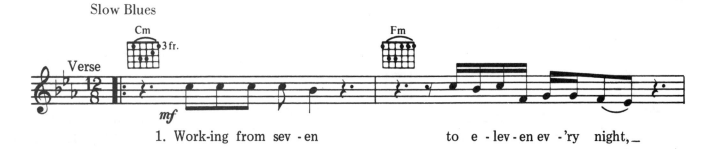

1. Work-ing from sev - en to e - lev-en ev -'ry night, __

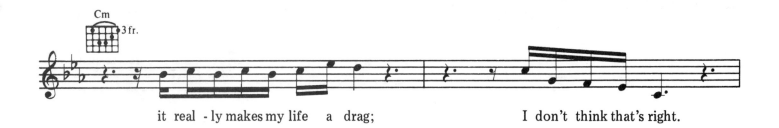

it real -ly makes my life a drag; I don't think that's right.

I've real -ly, real -ly been the best of fools, __ I did what I could, yeah,

'cause I love you, ba - by, how I love you, dar - ling, how I love you, ba - by,

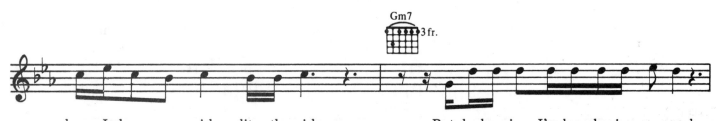

how I love you, girl, lit - tle girl. But ba-by, since I've been lov-ing you, yeah,

2. Everybody trying to tell me that you didn't mean me no good.
   I've been trying, Lord, let me tell you I really did the best I could.
   I've been working from seven to eleven every night; it kinda makes my life a drag.
   Lord, you know that ain't right.
   Since I've been loving you, I'm about to lose my worried mind.

Bridge

3. Do you remember, mama, when I knocked upon your door? I said you had the nerve to tell me
      you didn't want me no more.
   I open my front door, hear my back door slam; you know I must have one of them new-fangled,
      back-door man.
   I've been working from seven to eleven every night; it kinda makes my life a drag,
   A drag, drag, ah, yeah, it makes a drag.
   Since I've been loving you, I'm about to lose my worried mind.

TANGERINE

Words and Music by
JIMMY PAGE

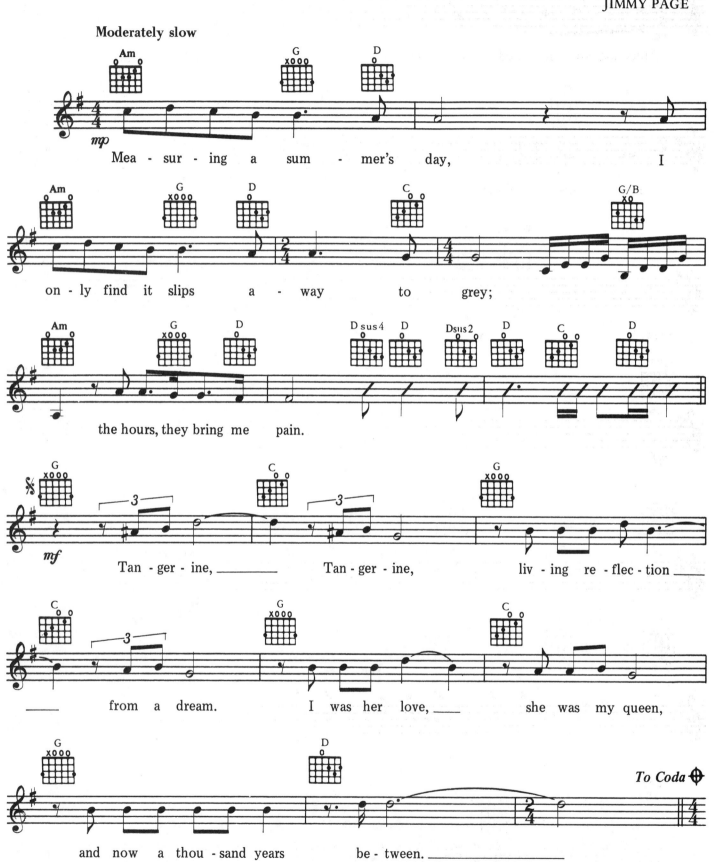

Think-ing how it used to be; does she still re-mem - ber

times like these to think of us a -

gain? And I do.

D. S. 𝄋 al Coda ⊕

Coda ⊕

rit.

GALLOWS POLE

Traditional
*Arrangement by JIMMY PAGE
and ROBERT PLANT*

Moderately

1. Hang - man,___ hang - man,___ hold it a lit - tle while,

think I see my friends com - ing, rid - ing man-y a mile.___

Friends, did you get some

sil - ver?___ Did you get a lit - tle gold? What did you

bring me, my dear___ friends, to keep me from the Gal - lows Pole?___

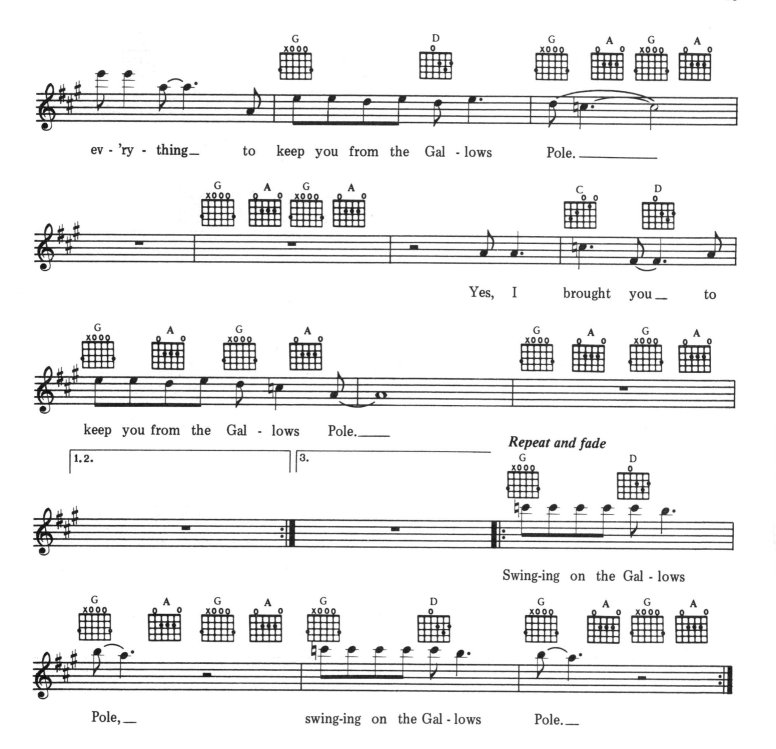

ev - 'ry - thing___ to keep you from the Gal - lows Pole.___

Yes, I brought you___ to

keep you from the Gal - lows Pole.___

1. 2.

3.

Repeat and fade

Swing-ing on the Gal - lows

Pole,___ swing-ing on the Gal - lows Pole.___

3. Hangman, hangman, turn your head awhile,
   I think I see my sister coming riding many a mile.
   Sister, I implore you, take him by the hand,
   Take him to some shady bower, save me from the wrath of this man.
   Please take him, save me from the wrath of this man.

4. Hangman, hangman, upon your face a smile,
   Pray tell me that I'm free to ride, ride for many a mile.
   Yes, you got a fine sister, she warmed my blood from cold,
   She brought my blood to boiling hot to keep you from the Gallows Pole.
   Your brother brought me silver, your sister warmed my soul,
   But now I laugh and pull so hard and see you swinging on the Gallows Pole.

OUT ON THE TILES

Words and Music by
JIMMY PAGE, ROBERT PLANT
and JOHN BONHAM

Moderate Rock beat

walk down the high-way all I do is sing this song, and a
I'm so glad I'm liv-in', gon-na tell the world I am, I

train that pass-es my way helps the rhy-thm move a-long._ There
got me a fine wom-an and she says that I'm her man._

is no doubt a - bout the words _ are clear, the voice _ is strong, is oh so
One thing that I know for sure, _ gonna give her all _ the lovin' like no - body

strong.
can.

I'm just a sim - ple guy and I
Stand - in' in the noonday sun,

live from day to day, _ a ray of sun - shine melts my frown _ and
try'n' to flag a ride, _ peo - ple go and peo - ple come, see my

blows my blues a - way. There's noth - ing more that I can say _ but on a
rider right by my side. It's a total dis - grace, they set the pace, _ it

FRIENDS

Words and Music by
JIMMY PAGE and ROBERT PLANT

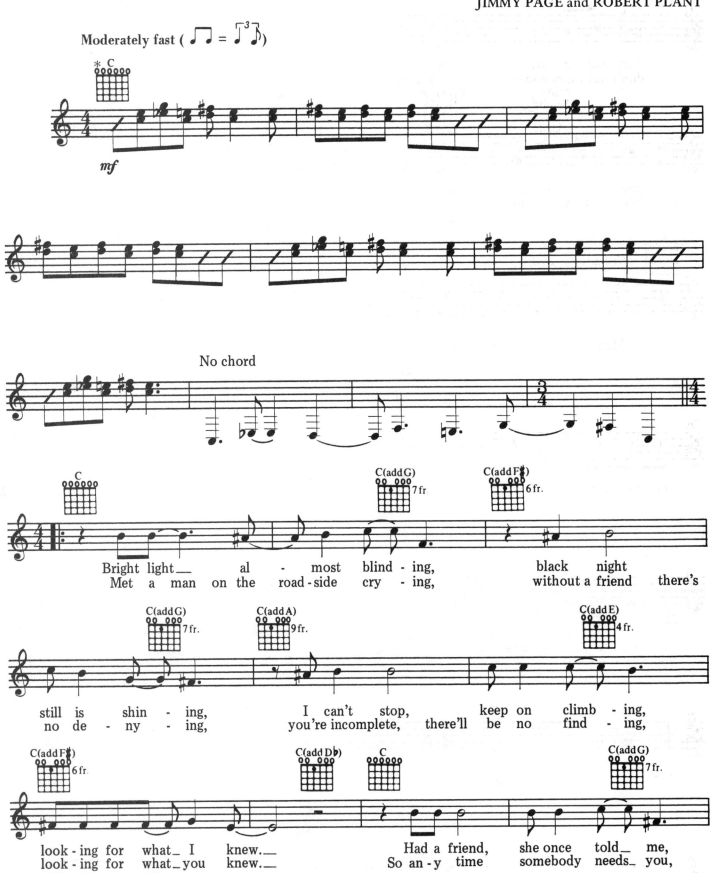

* Use open C tuning: CGCGCE.

"You got a love, you ain't lone - ly."
Now she's gone and left
don't let them down al - though it grieves you, someday you'll need some - one

me on - ly look - ing for what I knew.
like they do, look - ing for what you knew.

(Guitar as in Intro.)

Mm, I'm tell - ing you now, the great - est thing you

ev - er can do now, is trade a smile with some - one who's blue now,

N.C.

it's ver - y eas - y just.

1.

2.

C

HATS OFF TO (ROY) HARPER

Traditional
Arrangement by CHARLES OBSCURE

Brightly

1. When I done quit hol-ler-in', ba - by, I be - lieve ___ I'll shake 'em on down; get my babe ___ won't be late, ___ you know by that I mean sec - onds late. ___ Ah, must I hol - ler, ___

* Use open C tuning: CGCGCE.

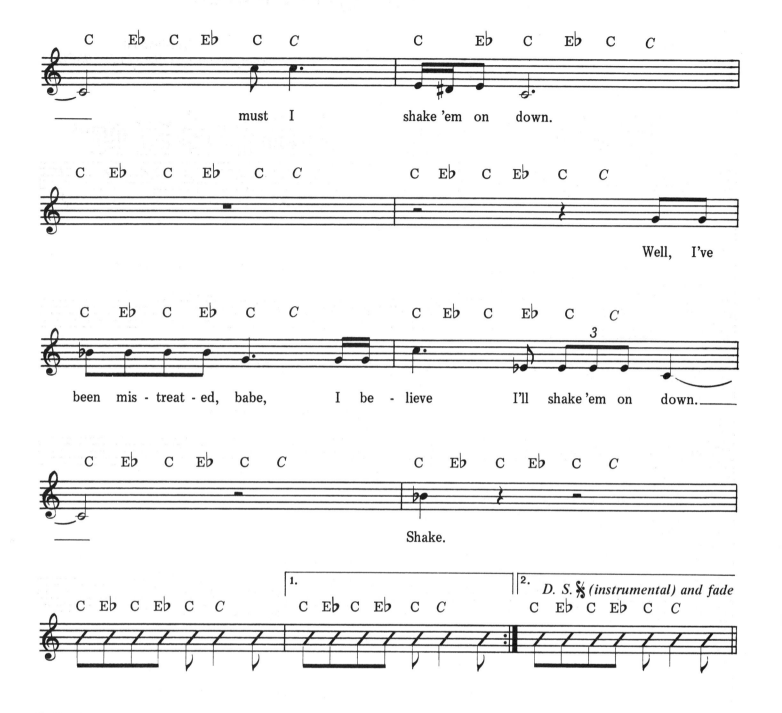

2. Well, I ain't no monkey, I can't climb no tree,
   No brown-skin woman gonna make no monkey out of me.
   I ain't no monkey, I can't climb no tree.
   I've been mistreated, babe, I believe I'll shake 'em on down.

3. Gave my baby a twenty-dollar bill,
   If that don't get her, sure my shotgun will.
   Yeah, I gave my baby a twenty-dollar bill,
   If that don't get that woman, I'm sure my shotgun will.

BRON-Y-AUR STOMP

Words and Music by
JIMMY PAGE, ROBERT PLANT
and JOHN PAUL JONES

Brightly

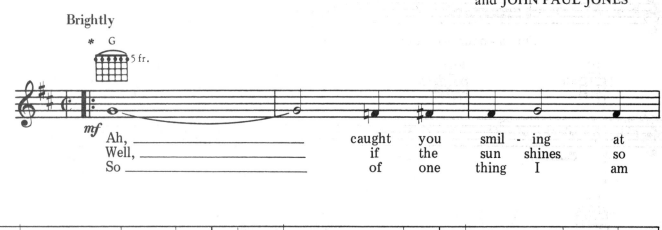

Ah, _____ caught you smil - ing at
Well, _____ if the sun shines so
So _____ of one thing I am

me, that's the way it should be, like a
bright, or our way, it's dark - est night, the road we
sure, it's a friend - ship so pure, an - gels

leaf is to a tree, so fine. _____
choose is al - ways right, so fine. _____
sing - ing all a - round my door so fine. _____

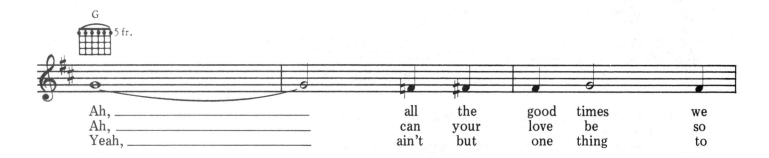

Ah, _____ all the good times we
Ah, _____ can your love be so
Yeah, _____ ain't but one thing to

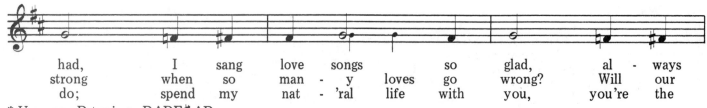

had, I sang love songs so glad, al - ways
strong when so man - y loves go wrong? Will our
do; spend my nat - 'ral life with you, you're the

* Use open D tuning: DADF♯AD.

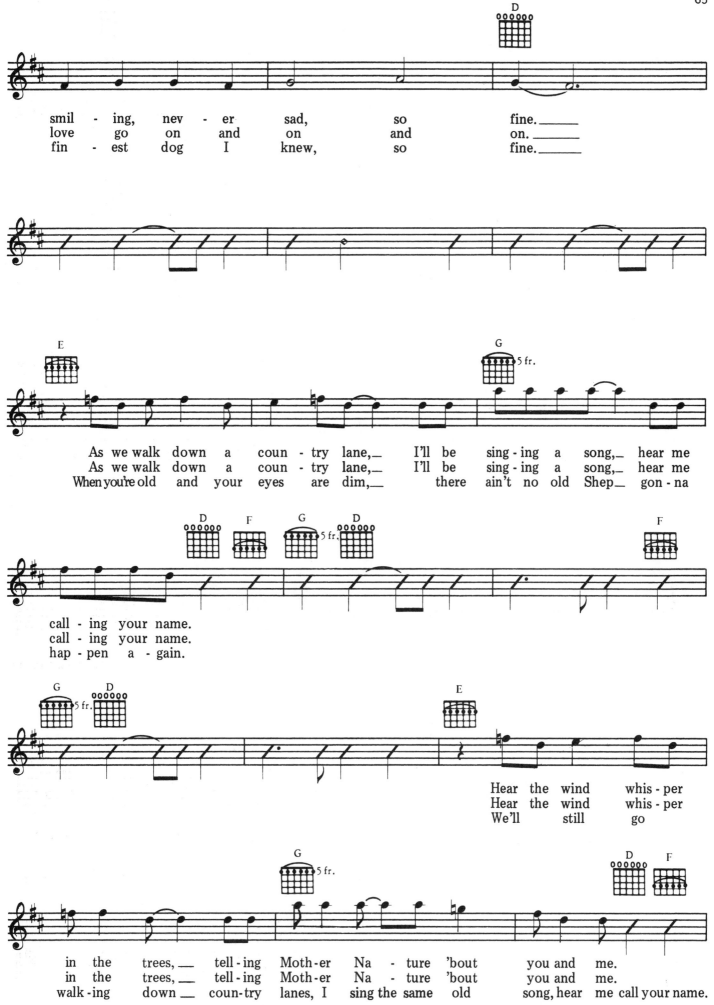

CELEBRATION DAY

Words and Music by
JIMMY PAGE, ROBERT PLANT
and **JOHN PAUL JONES**

Moderate Rock beat

1. Her

Verse *(Guitar simile)*

face is cracked from smil - ing,   all   the fears that she's been hid - ing,

and   it seems that pret-ty   soon   ev -'ry - bod - y's   gon - na   know. _____

And her

voice is sore from shout - ing, cheer - ing win - ners who are los - ing,

and she wor - ries if their days are few and soon ___ they'll have to

To Coda ⊕

go. _____

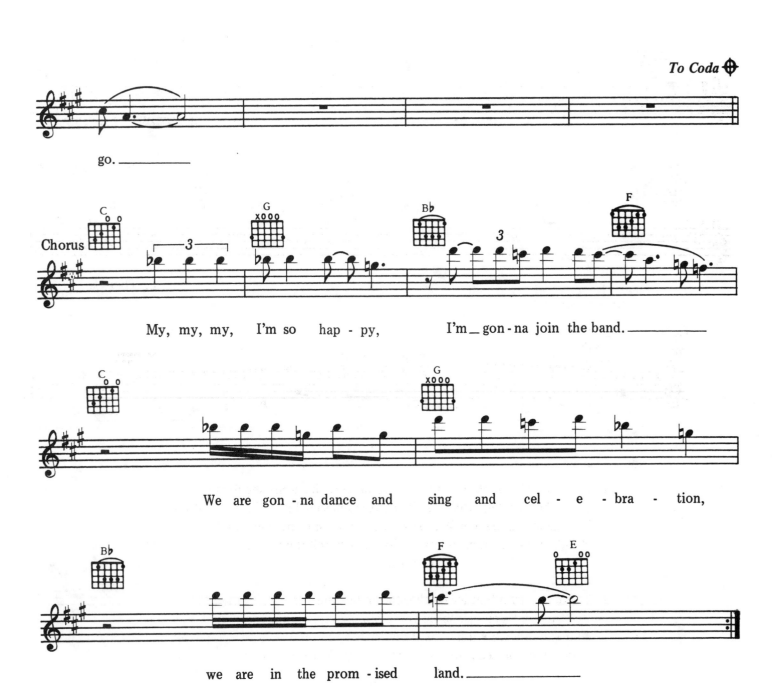

Chorus

My, my, my, I'm so hap - py, I'm ___ gon - na join the band. _____

We are gon - na dance and sing and cel - e - bra - tion,

we are in the prom - ised land. _____

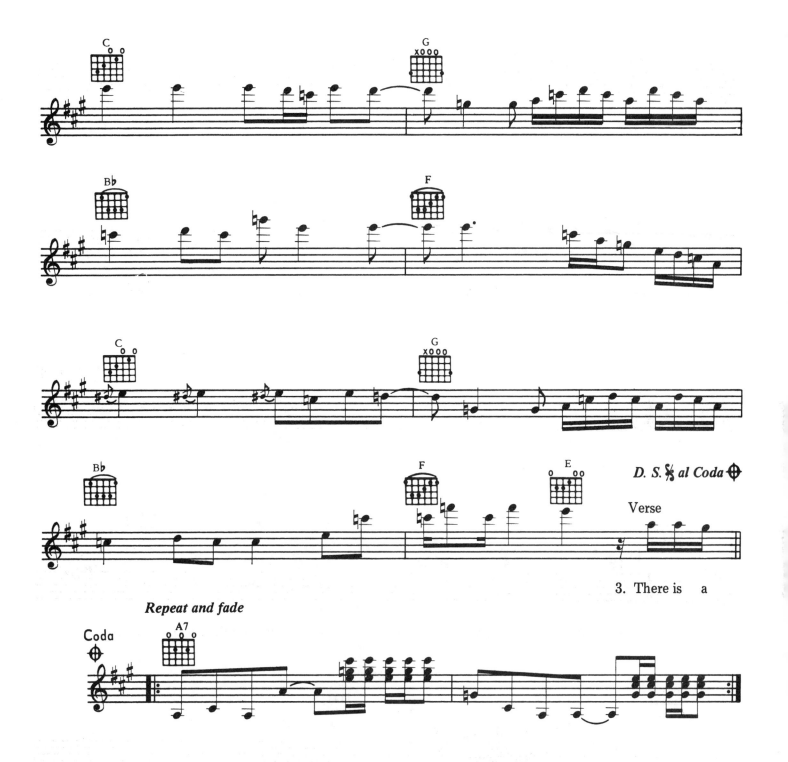

3. There is   a

2. She hears them talk of new ways to protect the home she lives in,
   Then she wonders what it's all about when they break down the door.
   Her name is Brown or White or Black; you know her very well.
   You hear her cries of mercy as the winners toll the bell.
   (Chorus)

3. There is a train that leaves the station heading for your destination,
   But the price you pay to nowhere has increased a dollar more. Yes, it has!
   And if you walk you're gonna get there although it takes a little longer,
   And when you see it in the distance you will wring your hands and moan.

LED ZEPPELIN IV

FOUR STICKS

Words and Music by
JIMMY PAGE and ROBERT PLANT

Oh, _____ ba - by, _____ it's cry - in' time; _____

oh, _____ ba - by, _____ I got to fly. _____

MISTY MOUNTAIN HOP

Words and Music by
JIMMY PAGE, ROBERT PLANT
and JOHN PAUL JONES

think I saw?_____

Crowds__ of peo - ple sit - tin' on the

grass with flow - ers in their hair said, "Hey, boy, do you__

__ wan-na score?"__ And you know how it is;

I real-ly don't know. _____

I real-ly don't

2. I didn't notice but it had got very dark and I was really
     really out of my mind.
 Just then a policeman stepped up to me and asked us, said, "Please, hey,
     would we care to all get in line, get in line."
 Well, you know, they asked us to stay for tea and have some fun; oh, oh,
     he said that his friends would all drop by.

3. Why don't you take a good look at yourself and describe what you see,
     and baby, baby, baby, do you like it?
 There you sit, sittin' spare like a book on a shelf rustin',
     ah, not tryin' to fight it.
 You really don't care if they're comin'; oh, oh,
     I know that it's all a state of mind.

4. If you go down in the streets today, baby, you better,
     you better open your eyes.
 Folk down there really don't care, really don't care, really don't, which way the pressure lies,
     so I've decided what I'm gonna do now.
 So I'm packin' my bags for the Misty Mountains where the spirits go now,
     over the hills where the spirits fly.

WHEN THE LEVEE BREAKS

Words and Music by
JIMMY PAGE, ROBERT PLANT,
JOHN PAUL JONES, JOHN BONHAM
and MEMPHIS MINNIE

have no   place __   to stay. _____
ma -ma,   you got   to move.__

Mean old   lev - ee ___   taught me   to   weep_ and   moan; ___
All last   night,_   sat on   the   lev - ee and   moaned; __

mean old   lev - ee __   taught me   to   weep_ and   moan.
all last   night,_   sat on   the   lev -ee and   moaned._

___   It's   got what it   takes_ to   make a
___   Think - in' 'bout my   ba - by   and

moun - tain man ___   leave his   home. __}   Oh, well, ___   oh, well, __   oh, well.
my hap -   py home. __}

Don't it make you feel bad when you're try-in' to find your way home, you

don't know_ which way to go?_____ If you're go-in' down South, they got

no work to do, if you don't know a-bout Chi - ca - go.

81

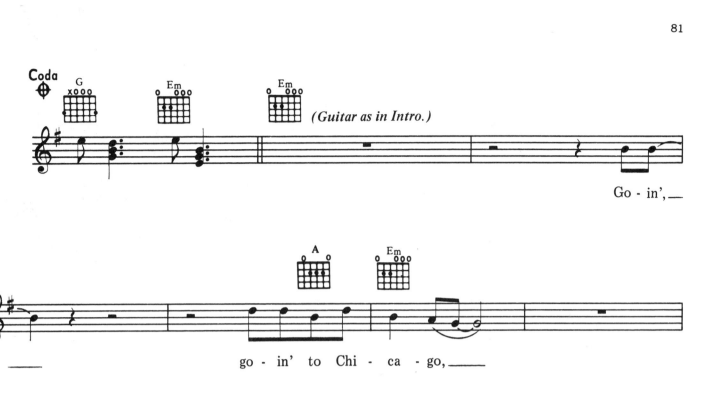

(Guitar as in Intro.)

Go - in', __

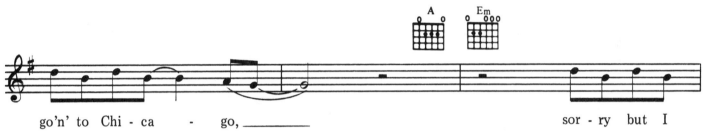

__ go - in' to Chi - ca - go, ____

go'n' to Chi - ca - go, _____ sor - ry but I

can't take you. _____ Go - ing down, go - ing

down now, go - ing down, go - ing down now, go - ing down.

Repeat and fade

BLACK DOG

Words and Music by
JIMMY PAGE, ROBERT PLANT
and JOHN PAUL JONES

hon - ey drip,__ can't keep a - way.__ }
big - leg - ged wom - an ain't got no soul.__ }

Ah, yeah, ah, yeah, ah, ah, ah.__

84

{ I got-ta roll,   can't stand still,   got a   flam - in'   heart,   can't
{ All I   ask   for,   all I   pray,   stead-y roll - in' wom-an gon - na

get my   fill.____
come my   way.____

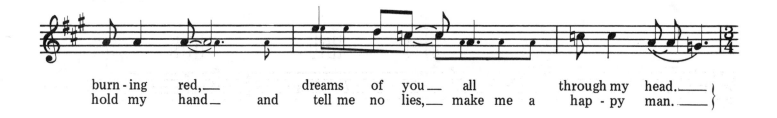

Eyes   that shine,__
Need a wom - an gon -na

burn - ing red,___   dreams of you__ all   through my head.__ }
hold my hand__   and   tell me no lies,__ make me a   hap - py man. __ }

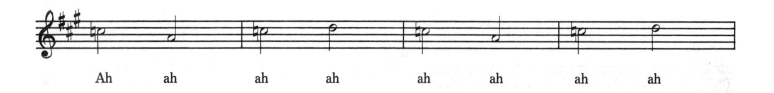

Ah   ah   ah   ah   ah   ah   ah   ah

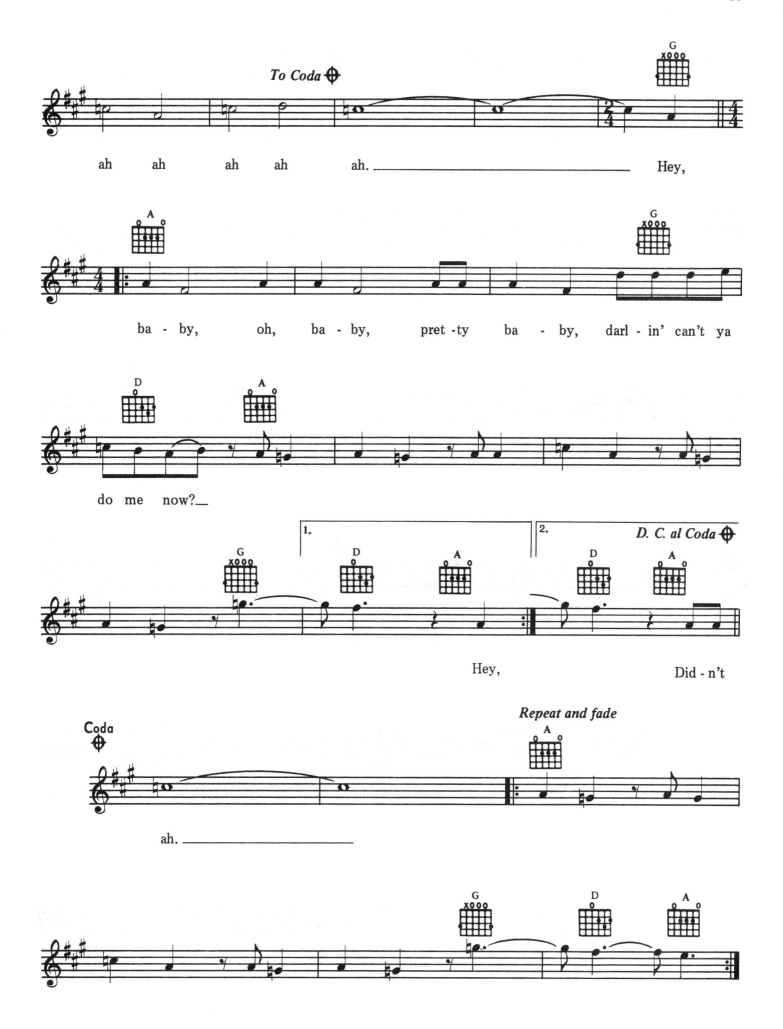

STAIRWAY TO HEAVEN

Words and Music by
JIMMY PAGE and **ROBERT PLANT**

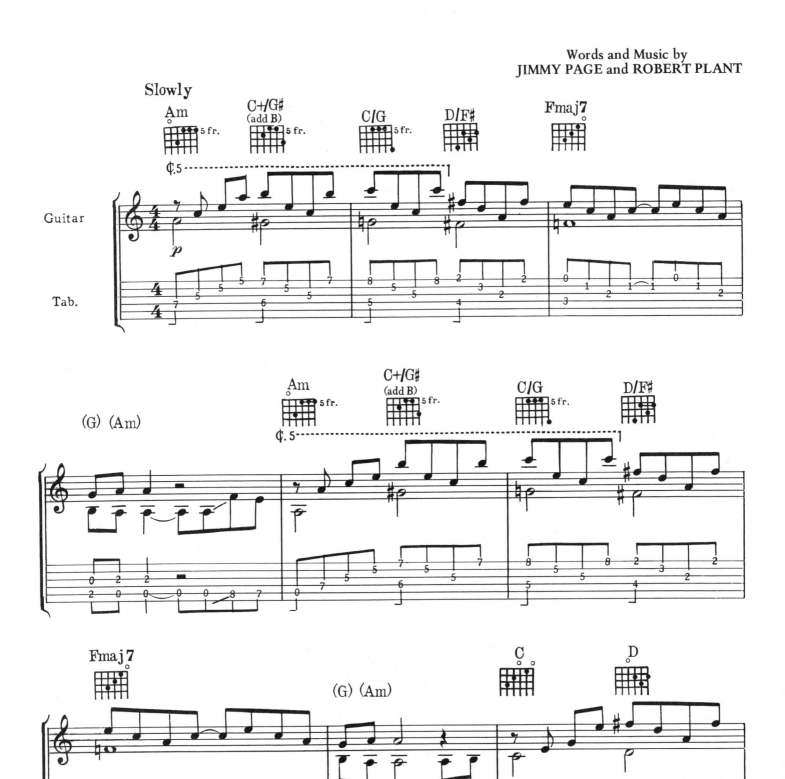

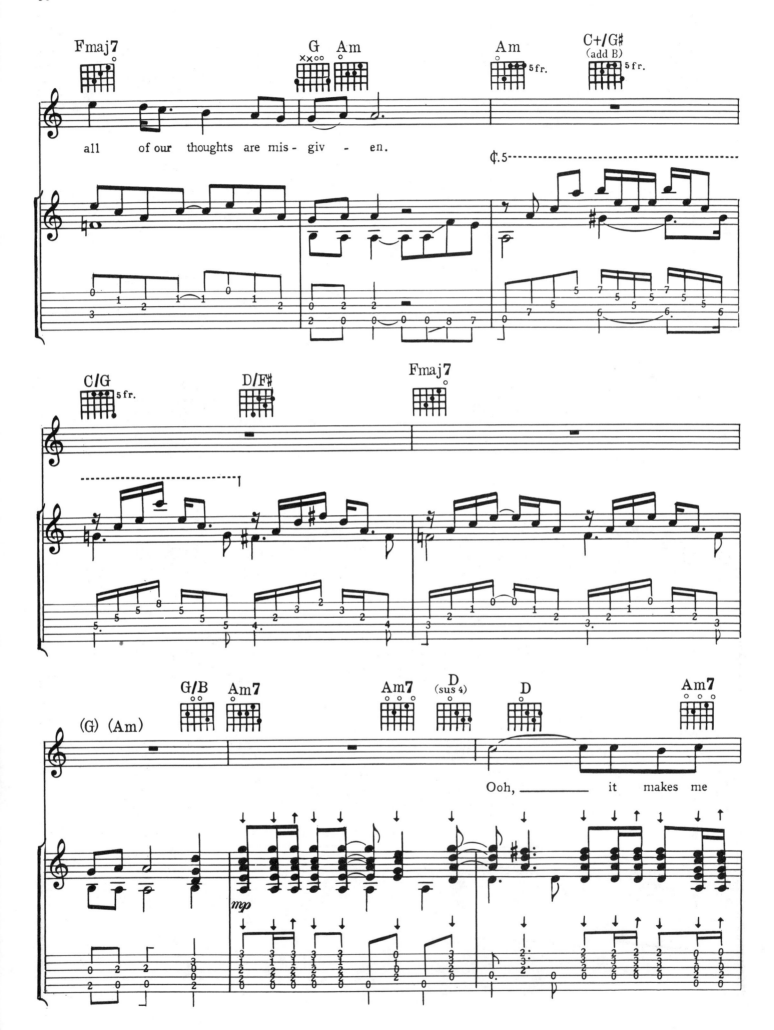

91

new day will dawn___ for those who stand long___ and the for - ests will ech - o with laugh-

ter.

Wo___wo___wo___ wo _____
(2nd time only)

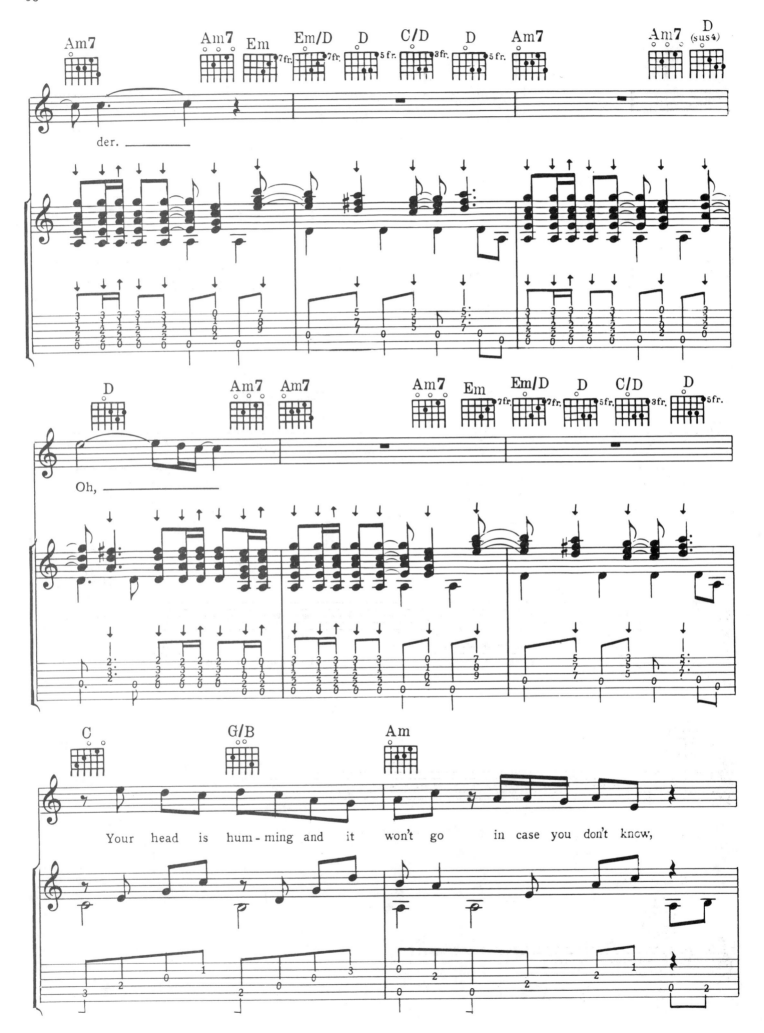

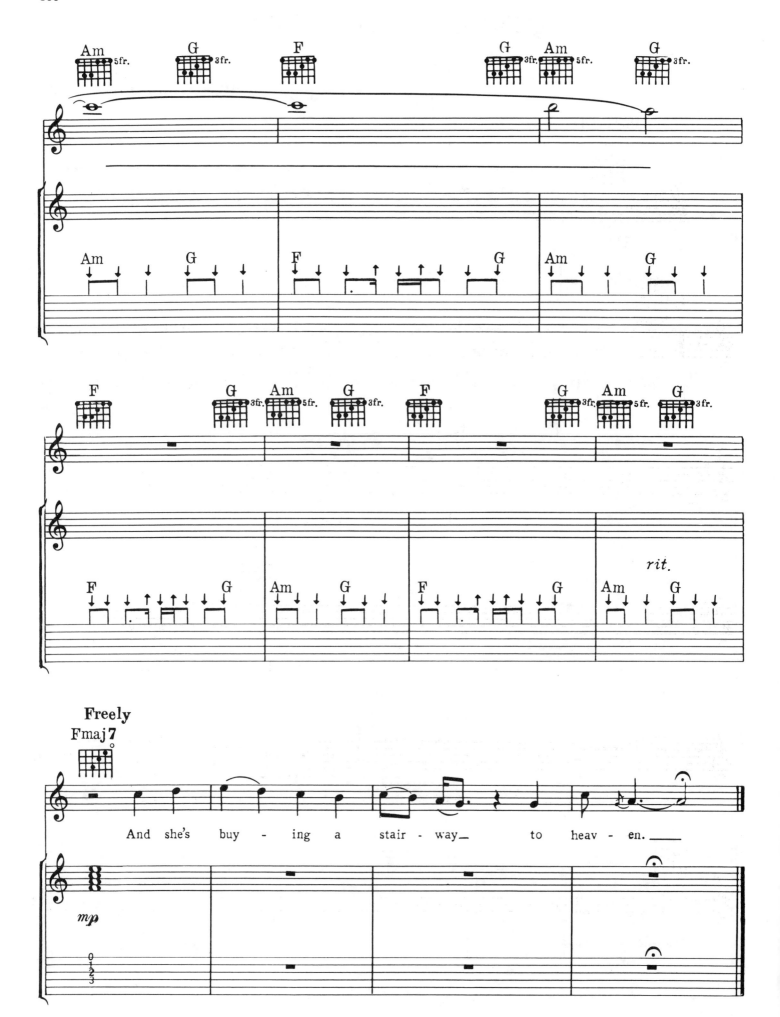

And she's buy-ing a stair-way___ to heav-en.___

GOING TO CALIFORNIA

Words and Music by
JIMMY PAGE and **ROBERT PLANT**

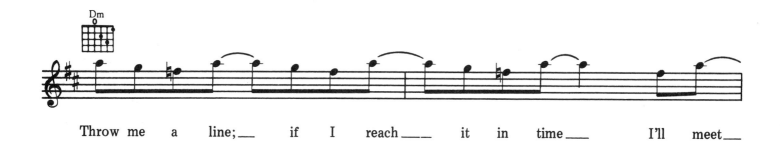

Throw me a line;___ if I reach___ it in time___ I'll meet___

___ you up there___ where the path___ runs___ straight___ and

D. S. 𝄋 al Coda ⊕
Verse

high. _____

To

Repeat and fade

Coda ⊕

2. Took my chances on a big jet plane,
   Never let 'em tell you that they're all the same.
   Sea was red and the sky was grey,
   Wondered how tomorrow could ever follow today.
   The mountains and the canyons start to tremble and shake.
   The children of the sun begin to awake.

Bridge

3. To find a queen without a king;
   They say she plays guitar and cries and sings.
   Ride a white mare in the footsteps of dawn.
   Trying to find a woman who's never been born.
   Standing on a hill in my mountain of dreams,
   Telling myself that it's not as hard as it seems.

ROCK AND ROLL

Words and Music by
JIMMY PAGE, ROBERT PLANT,
JOHN PAUL JONES and JOHN BONHAM

Medium Rock beat

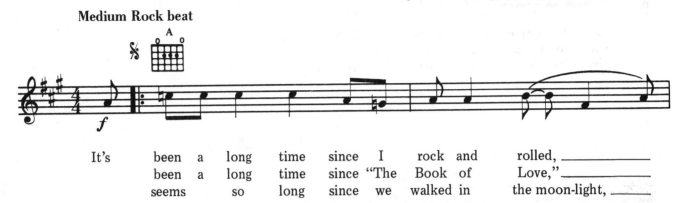

It's been a long time since I rock and rolled, _____
been a long time since "The Book of Love," _____
seems so long since we walked in the moon-light, _____

it's been a long time since I
I can't count the tears of a
mak - in' vows that

did the stroll. _____
life with no love. _____
just can't work _ right. _____

Let me get it back, let me get it back, let me get it back,
Car - ry me back, car - ry me back, car - ry me back,
O - pen your arms, o - pen your arms, o - pen your arms,

ba - by, where I ____ come from. _____
ba - by, where I ____ come from. _____
ba - by let my love come run - ning in.

It's been a long time, been a

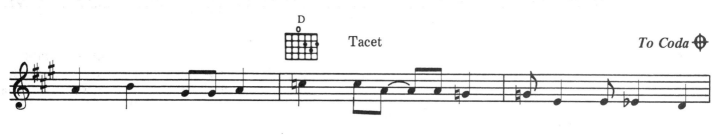

Tacet   *To Coda* ⊕

long time, been a long, lone - ly, lone - ly, lone - ly, lone - ly, lone - ly

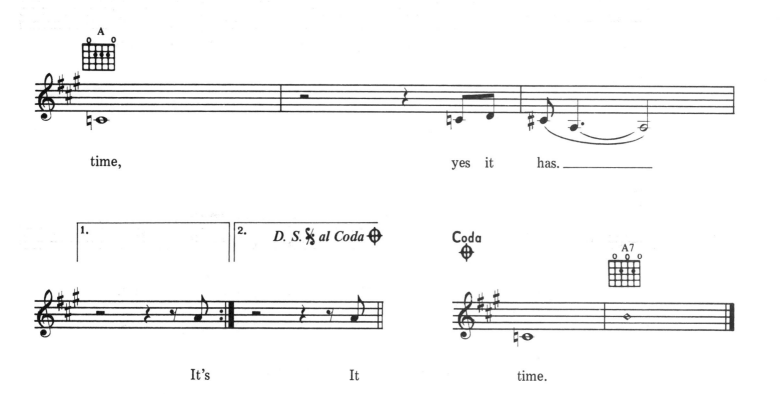

time,   yes it has. _____

1.   **2.** *D. S.* 𝄋 *al Coda* ⊕   **Coda** ⊕

It's   It   time.

THE BATTLE OF EVERMORE

Words and Music by
JIMMY PAGE and ROBERT PLANT

108

LED ZEPPELIN V

THE CRUNGE

Words and Music by
JOHN BONHAM, JOHN PAUL JONES,
JIMMY PAGE and ROBERT PLANT

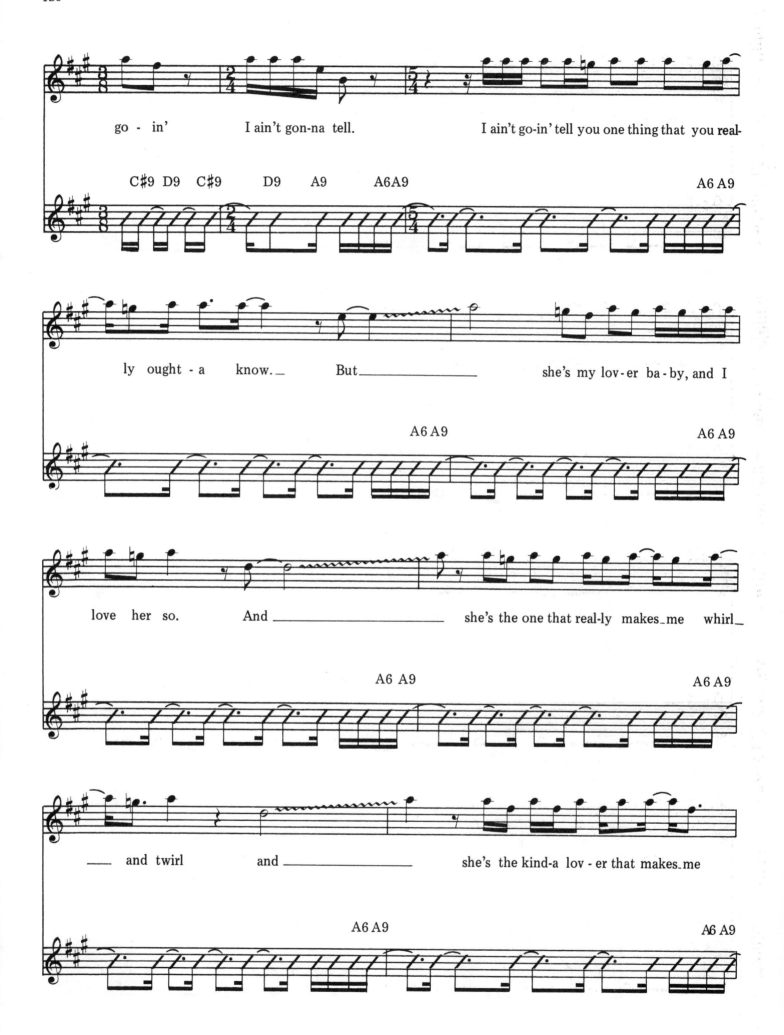

D'YER MAK'ER

Words and Music by
JOHN BONHAM, JOHN PAUL JONES
and ROBERT PLANT

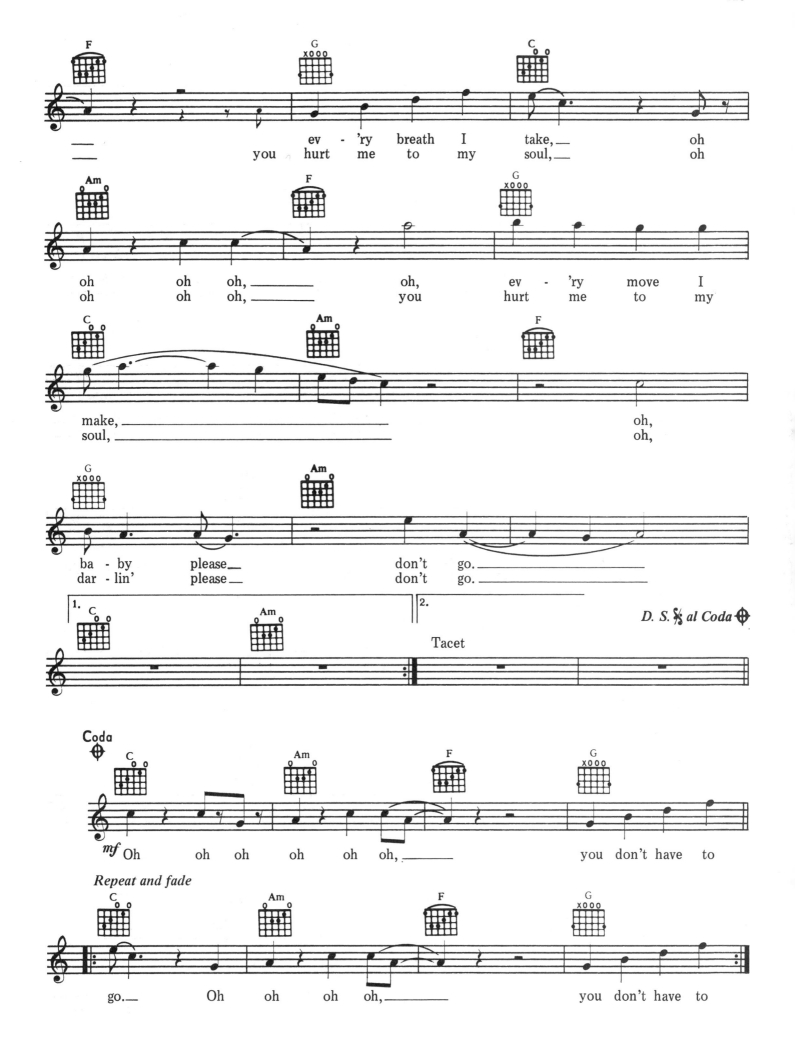

OVER THE HILLS AND FAR AWAY

Words and Music by
JIMMY PAGE and ROBERT PLANT

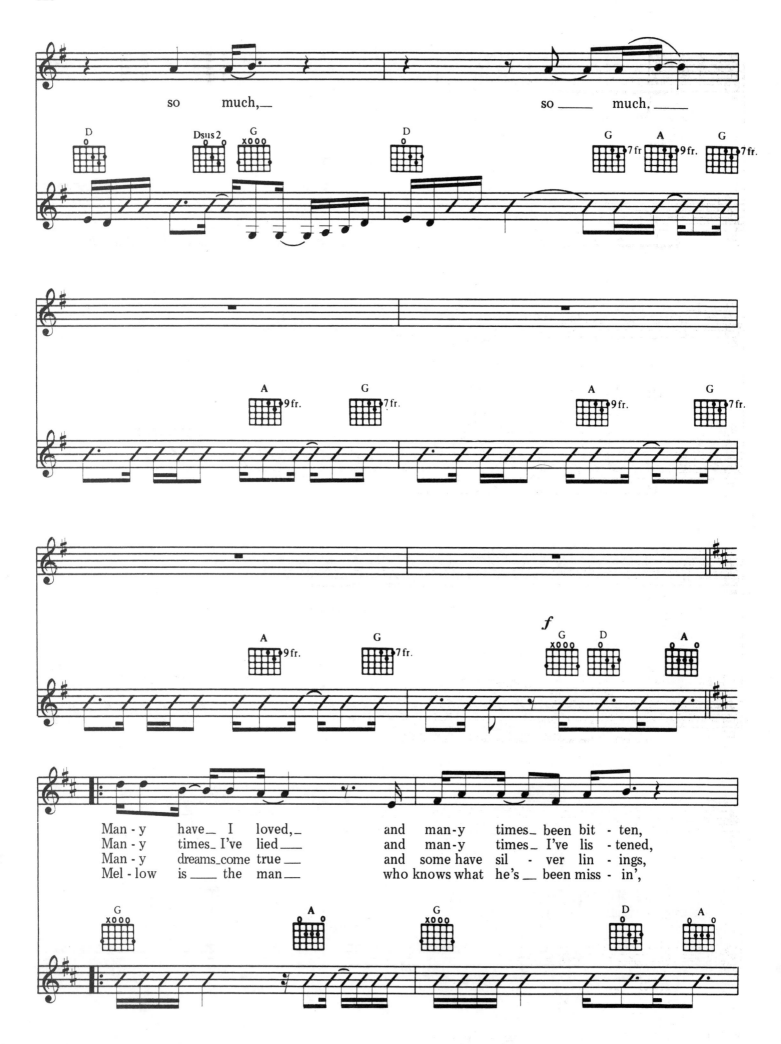

so   much,___   so ___ much.___

Man - y   have_ I   loved,_   and   man-y   times_   been   bit - ten,
Man - y   times_ I've   lied___   and   man-y   times_ I've   lis - tened,
Man - y   dreams_come   true ___   and   some   have   sil - ver   lin - ings,
Mel - low   is ___ the   man ___   who   knows   what   he's __ been   miss - in',

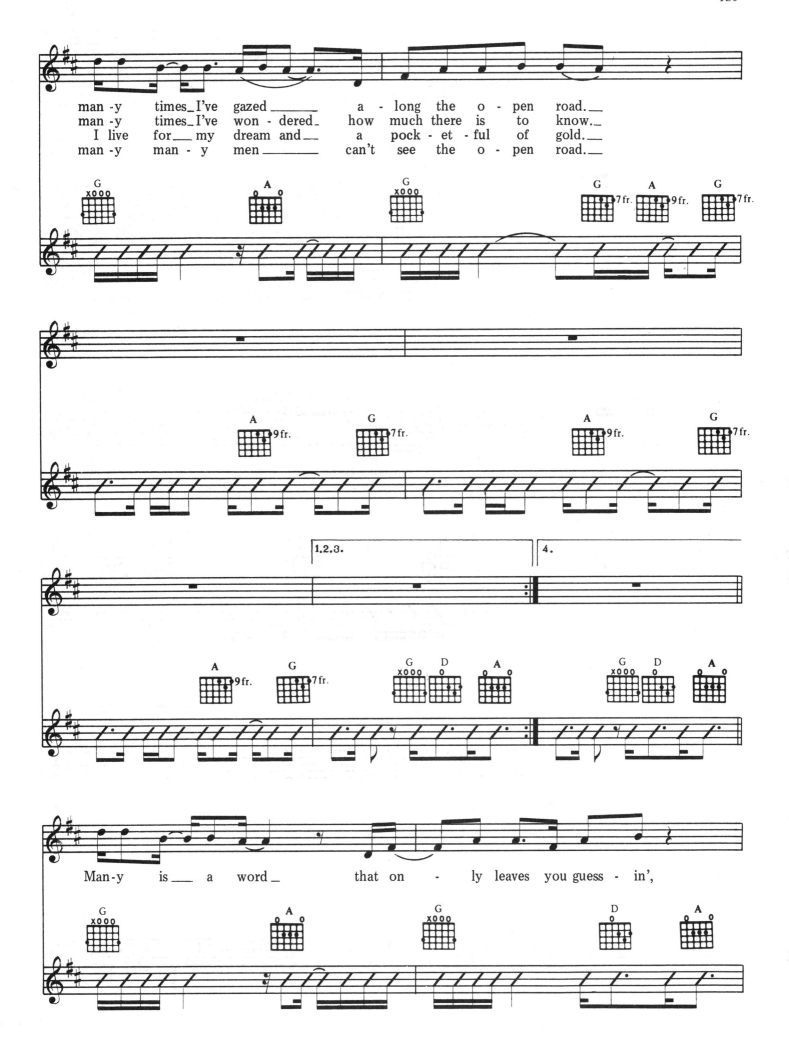

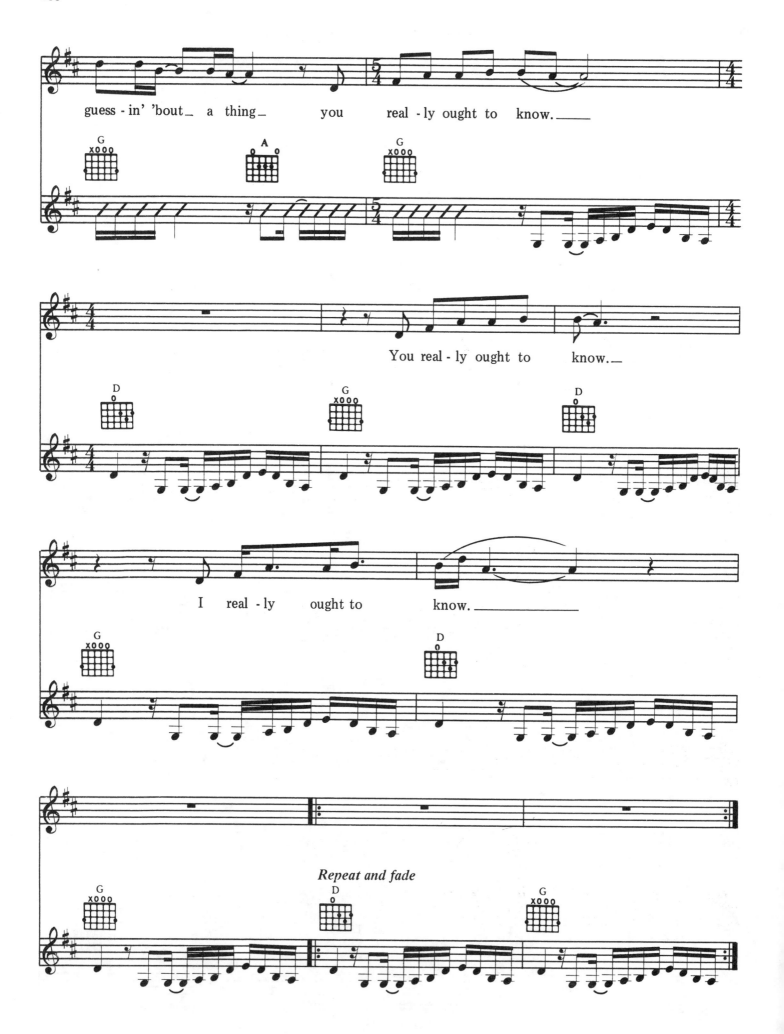

THE RAIN SONG

Words and Music by
JIMMY PAGE and ROBERT PLANT

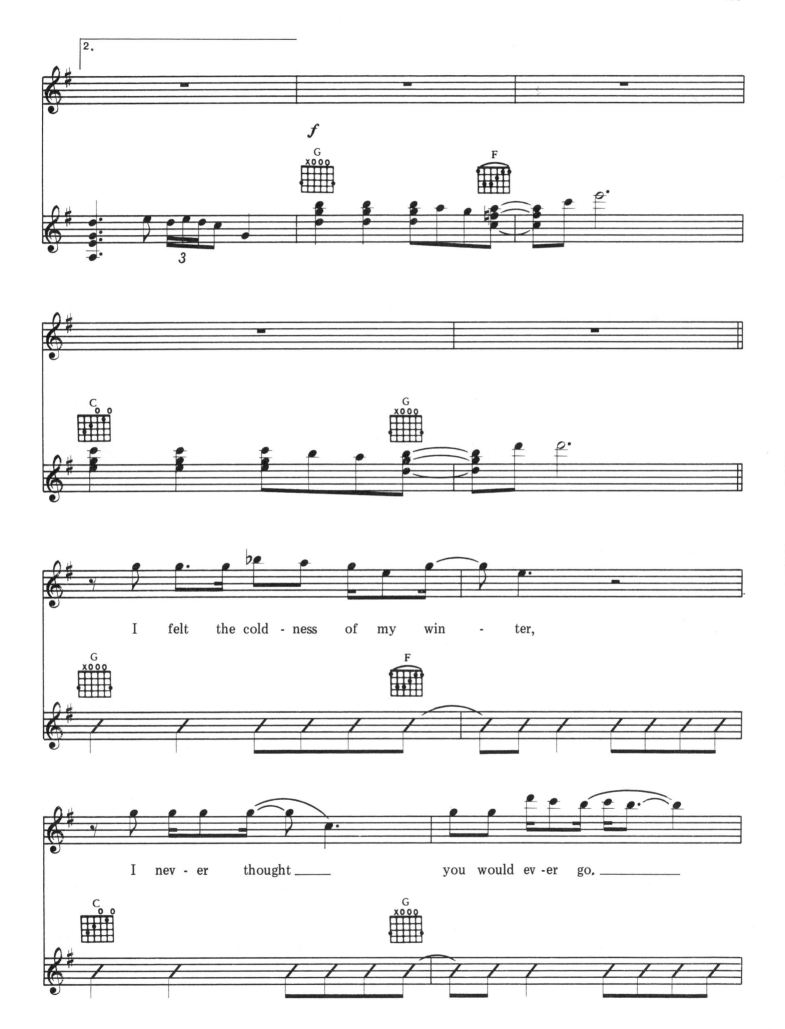

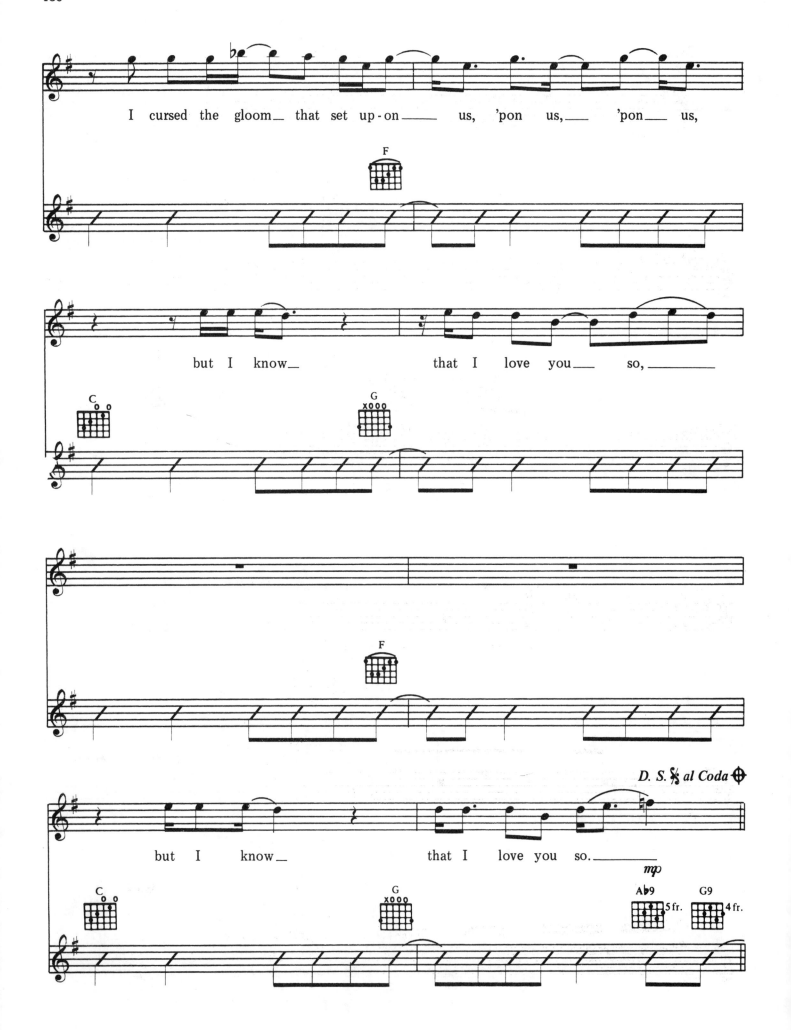

NO QUARTER

Words and Music by
JOHN PAUL JONES, JIMMY PAGE
and ROBERT PLANT

Moderately slow

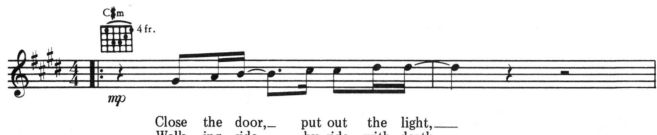

Close the door,___ put out the light,___
Walk - ing side___ by side with death___

you know___ they won't___ be home to - night.___
the dev - il mocks___ their ev - 'ry step.___

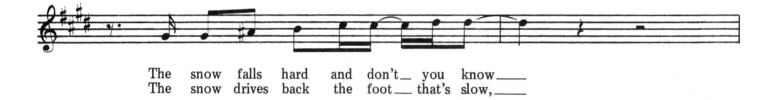

The snow falls hard and don't___ you know___
The snow drives back the foot___ that's slow,___

the winds of Thor___ are blow - ing cold.
the dogs of doom___ are howl - ing more.

They're wear - ing steel___ that's bright___ and true,_____
They car - ry news___ that must___ get through _____

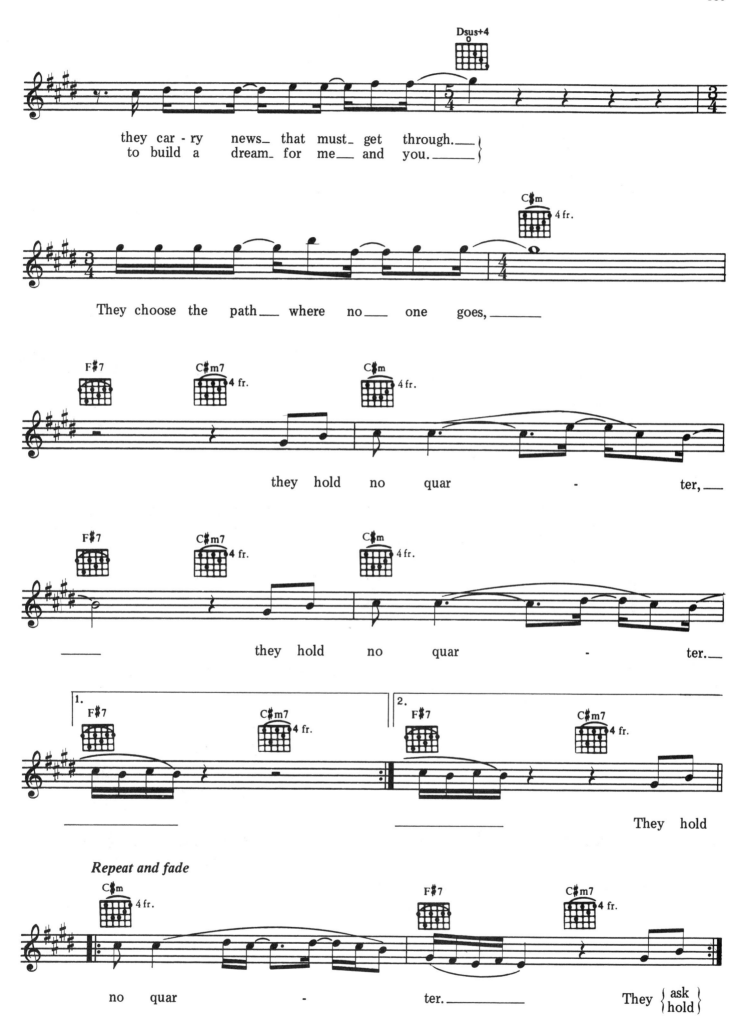

DANCING DAYS

Words and Music by
JIMMY PAGE and ROBERT PLANT

Moderately, with a beat

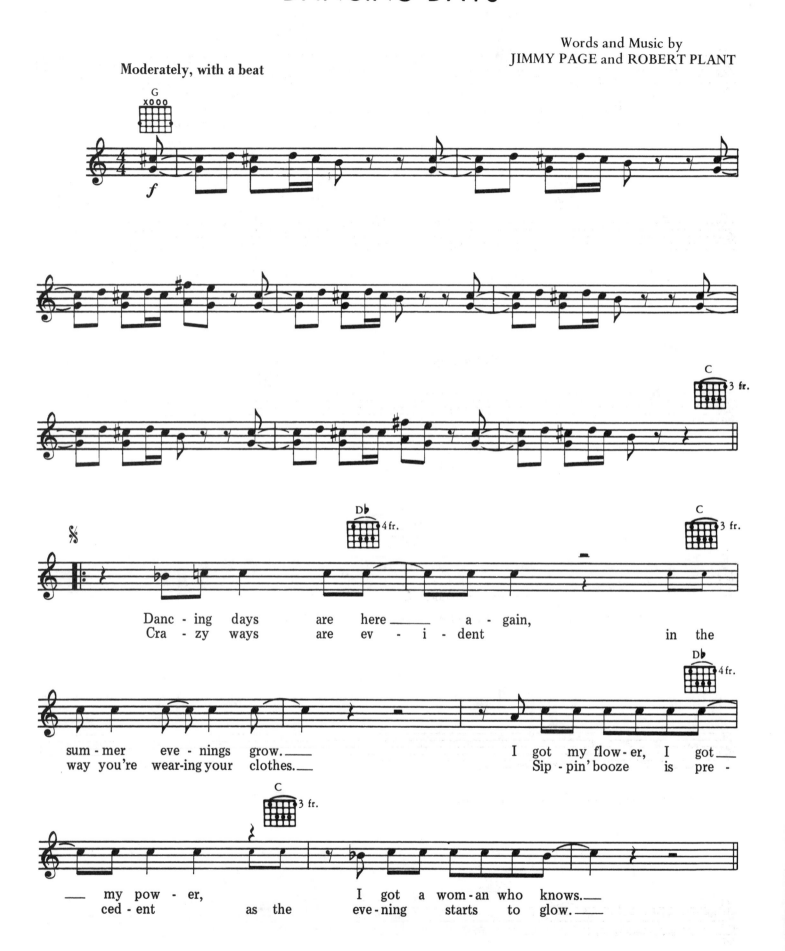

Danc - ing days are here ____ a - gain,
Cra - zy ways are ev - i - dent ____ in the

sum - mer eve - nings grow. ____ I got my flow - er, I got ____
way you're wear-ing your clothes. ____ Sip - pin' booze is pre -

____ my pow - er, I got a wom - an who knows. ____
ced - ent as the eve - ning starts to glow. ____

141

THE OCEAN

Words and Music by
JOHN BONHAM, JOHN PAUL JONES,
JIMMY PAGE and ROBERT PLANT

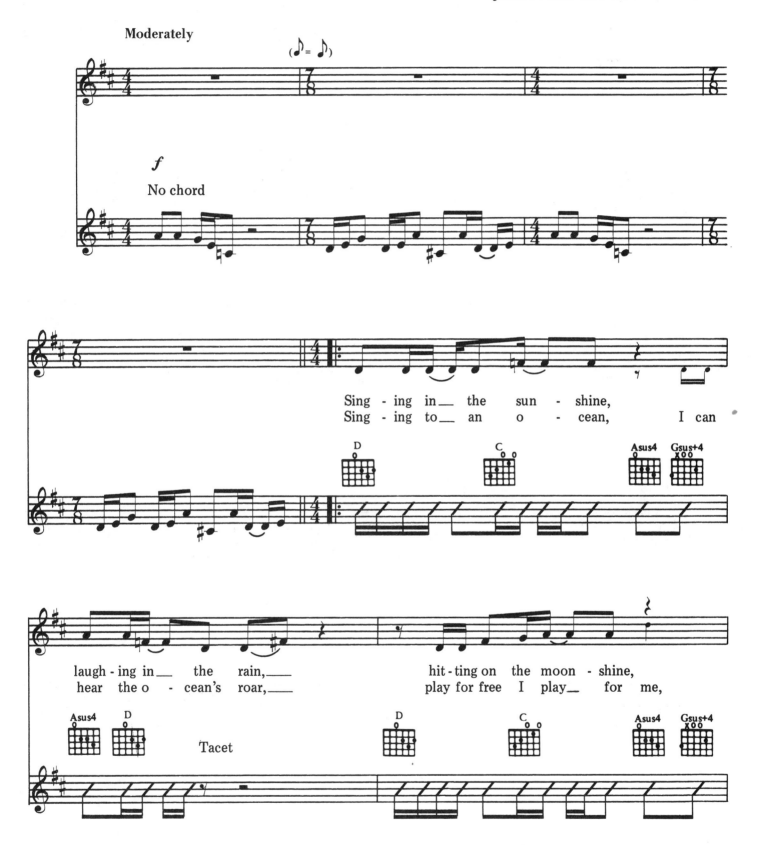

la la la la la la la _____ la la la la la la la la.

Sit - ting round,_ sing - ing songs_ till the night turns in - to day,_____

D C Asus4 Gsus+4 Asus4 D

Tacet

used to sing on the moun - tains, but the moun - tains washed a - way._

D C Asus4 Gsus+4 Asus4 D

Tacet

Now I'm sing - ing all_ my songs_ to the girl who won my heart,_

D C Asus4 Gsus+4 Asus4 D

Tacet

she is on-ly three years old _ and it's a real fine way to start. _____

Tacet

N.C.

THE SONG REMAINS THE SAME

Words and Music by
JIMMY PAGE and ROBERT PLANT

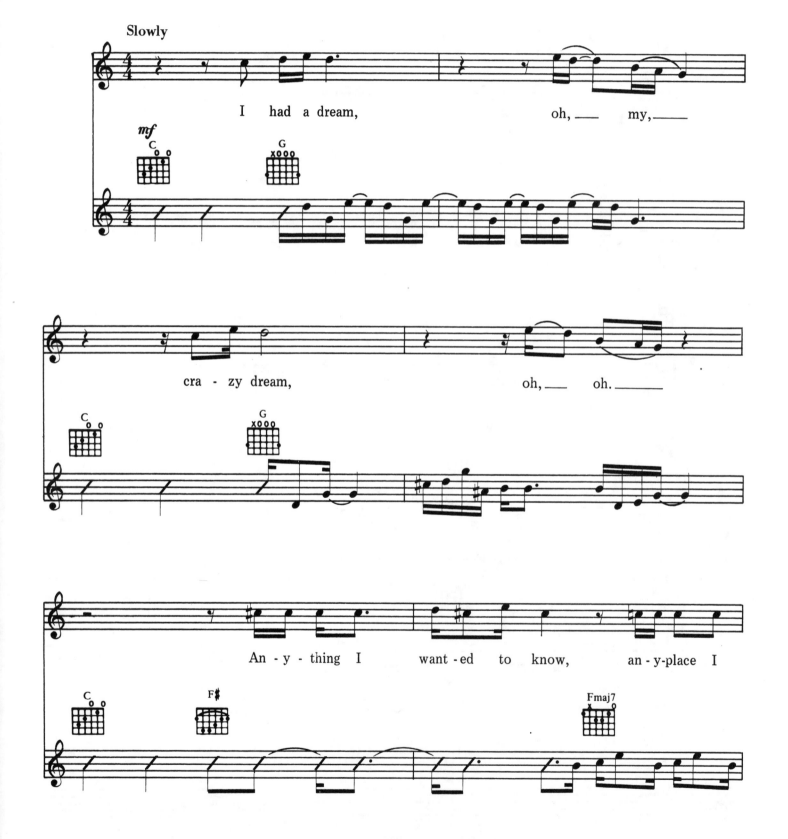

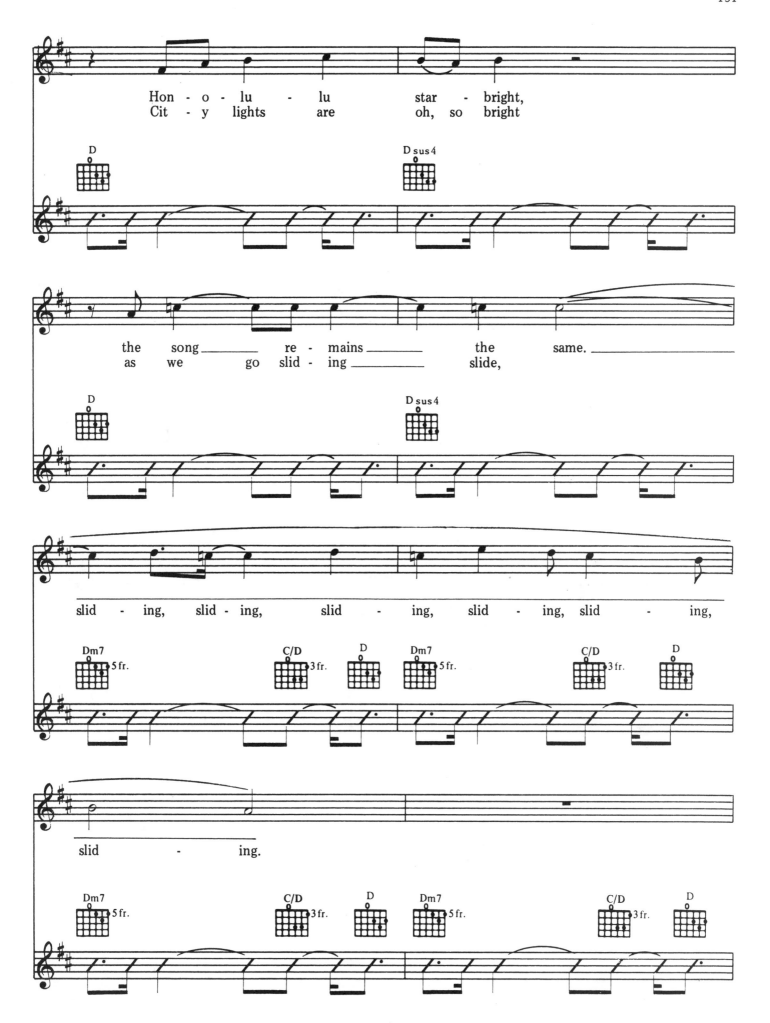

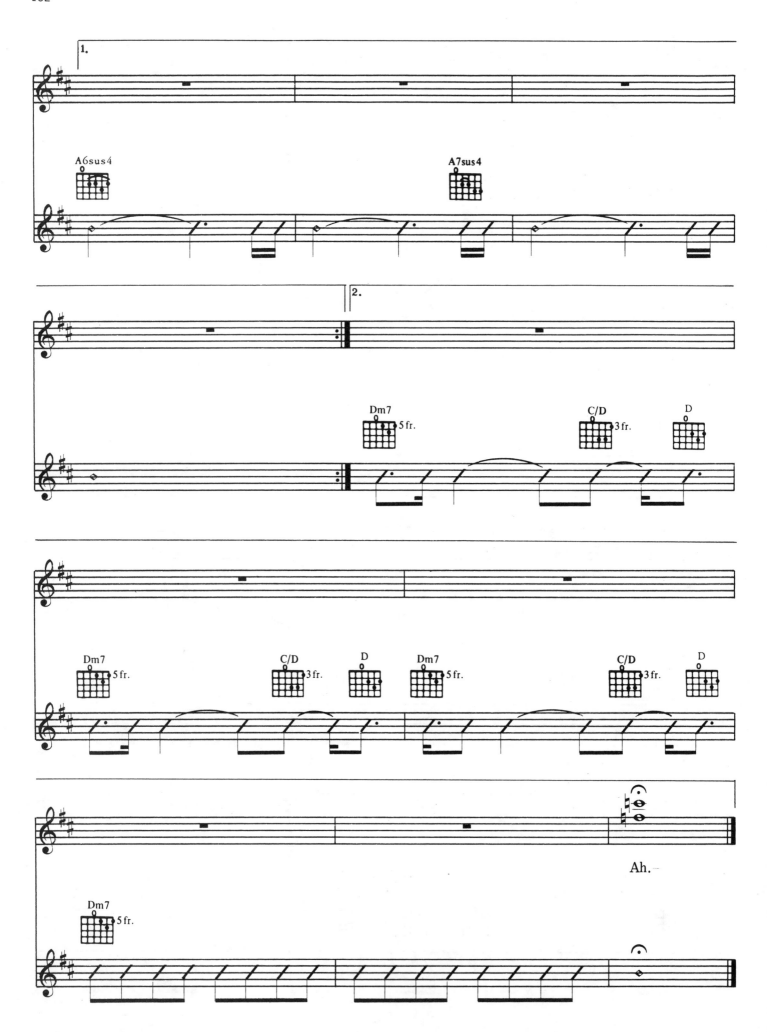

Ah. —